METHODS OF TEACHING
RELIGION TO CHILDREN

METHODS OF TEACHING RELIGION TO CHILDREN

FOR PARENTS AND TEACHERS

BY

MARJORIE E. A. CLARK

*Educational Secretary, Church of England Council
for Education Study Centre*

LONDON
NATIONAL SOCIETY
S · P · C · K
1956

First published in 1946 by the National Society
Reprinted, 1946, 1947, 1950

Revised edition published in 1956
by National Society and S.P.C.K.
Northumberland Avenue, London, W.C.2

Printed in Great Britain by
The Talbot Press (S.P.C.K.), Saffron Walden, Essex

PREFACE

THIS little book, intended in the first instance for the use of young, inexperienced teachers of children attending Sunday Schools and similar organizations for training in Christian faith and life, deserves a far wider public. There are now a great number of books on Child-study approached from a variety of angles and a certain number of books on methods of teaching religion. There has been, however, a very real need for a document which will bring the two subjects together, relating at every point what is known about the needs of children to the various means which have been discovered of transmitting truths of eternal value to young minds at the moment they are ready to receive them.

The writer has a certain amount of experience of children of all ages in school but a much greater and really intimate experience of children in their homes. She has the patient mind which is ready to listen and watch and the reverence and good sense which avert the catastrophe of over hasty conclusions. The book is freely illustrated by actual happenings in child life, and one realizes how precisely the methods indicated would help the children in the solution of their problems while stimulating their young minds to further endeavour and inquiry.

I should like to see this book used as material for study and discussion by a group composed of parents and teachers. If these two bodies of people would work together in the matter of the religious training of children much of the conflict in child life which is so disturbing to the process of growth in the life of religion could be avoided.

CATHARINE R. NEWBY
(formerly Principal of St Christopher's College, Blackheath)
September, 1944.

INTRODUCTION

THIS book, originally designed as a handbook for teachers engaged in the voluntary religious education of children, has now been revised and brought up to date. It is hoped that it may also prove useful to others, including parents and day school teachers, who are responsible for the religious training of the children in their care.

The book is intentionally simple, and few technical terms have been used, as it is intended, primarily, for those who have little leisure or opportunity for deeper study. While for those to whom the subject is already familiar, it may be helpful to break away from the purely academic treatment, and to consider it in a more homely way.

As the book is written with teachers in mind, frequent reference is made to "the teacher", "schools", and "departments", and the various methods are described as for class teaching. But the greater part of these methods could easily be adapted for use with any small group of children, or even with one child alone.

Knowledge of methods, however, is not sufficient in itself, the reasons for them must be known and understood. A visitor was once asked to visit a Sunday Kindergarten and to give the teachers some help. It was being run by three keen, young teachers, who had inherited the school from a succession of superintendents, back and back to the founder who was, at that time, extremely up-to-date, and had introduced all the approved equipment. One of the teachers superintended, one played the piano, and the third looked after the children, who sat on small, folding "deck" chairs. There was a superintendent's table, on which stood very correctly a Birthday Candle Stand filled with candles. At the end of the afternoon the visitor asked why no Birth-days had been kept, since the stand had been put out, and discovered that the teachers had no idea what the stand was for, or that it could be used. It was there when they came, and had always stood in the same place, and was regarded as part of the proper furniture of a Kindergarten, but that was all!

In order that the methods recommended in the book can be used intelligently, a brief study of the children we teach is included: their interests, from which we can discover the form our teaching should take in order to meet their needs at each stage of their development; and their charac-teristics, from which we can learn the best methods by which that teaching can be given.

Throughout the book the masculine personal pronoun for both teacher and child has generally been used, to avoid a frequent use of the awkward "him or her". But in most cases it should be understood that the terms "the teacher", "the Junior Child", etc., are intended to include both men and women, and girls as well as boys.

The various age-groups are named in accordance with the provisions of the 1944 Education Act. For children in the age-groups under eleven, education is provided in Primary Schools; for those over eleven it is provided in Secondary Grammar, Secondary Modern, or Secondary Technical Schools.

Much valuable help in the revision of this book has been given by Miss M. M. Bostock, Field Secretary, Church of England Council for Education Children's Council.

CONTENTS

CHAPTER 1

THE NEED FOR METHOD IN TEACHING

THE need for method in teaching is much the same as the need for method in doing anything else that is worth while, from sweeping a room to governing a country. For either of these, two things are necessary, if they are to be done well —a Purpose and a Plan. If we do not know *why* a room should be swept—that is, if we see no purpose in sweeping it —then we shall not be likely to do it well. Again, if we do not know *how* to set about the task, we shall only succeed in muddling through it. So it is with teaching : we not only need to know *why* we are going to teach, but must also have a plan of *how* we are going to do it—otherwise we shall only muddle through.

This is necessary for any kind of teaching. It is absolutely essential when we are going to teach what is not only the most important subject of all, but also the one that should have the deepest and most lasting influence upon the children we teach. Teachers of religion must, therefore, study most carefully the various methods of teaching.

And the methods are very varied. There are some teachers of religion who seem to take it for granted that there is one, and only one, method that may be used. Week by week there is exactly the same programme. The prayers may vary a little, different hymns will be sung, and the lesson will change from week to week; but the *method* remains the same from year to year, and the school, however orderly, seems lifeless. The children go through the same routine from the time of their entry into the school, at the age of five

1   2*

or even younger, until they leave, and it is small wonder if they break away from organized religion as soon as they have left school.

Yet even in ordinary, everyday life we should not dream of using the same method to teach any particular thing to children of different ages, abilities, or circumstances.

Let us think for a moment of a very simple illustration. Picture, for example, the many ways in which a town child might be taught about life on a farm. No doubt, long before he can walk or talk, he will have been given a picture-book of farmyard animals, with no printed matter in it at all. First he will enjoy the colours; then, when he is able to distinguish between the different animals, he will be taught the various noises which the animals make, and learn to make them even before he can say their names. As he gets older other uses can be made of this same book. Stories can be made up about the animals, and the child brought into the stories. Then, of course, there will be illustrated story-books to be read to the child, until he can begin to read them for himself. Perhaps someone who grew up on a farm will tell him real stories of "when she was a little girl". Some of the educational films and radio talks give information about farm life; the child can be given a toy model farm, and encouraged to add to it; best of all, he can be taken to spend a summer holiday on, or near, a farm.

These various methods could be used to teach almost any subject, and they, as well as many others, can all be used in one form or another by the teacher of religion. And their use brings delight to both teacher and children, and will ensure for the latter that the memories of their early religious teaching will be happy ones.

Teaching is really a sharing of something that we have with someone who has less than we have, or none at all. All our life we are doing this—offering advice, giving information, sharing experiences; and in doing so we use many methods. We bring back snaps from our holidays to show our friends; we seize paper and pencil and make a rough sketch or diagram to help an explanation; we perform ourselves an action we want to describe; we ask our friends to handle, taste, smell, as well as to see and listen; and the greater our desire to share, the more successful will be our methods of sharing.

It would now be helpful to think out a few quite ordinary things that we might want to "teach" other people, and how we could set about doing it. The following questions should be dealt with very simply. First a real situation must be imagined, where possible with some one we know quite well, and then we can consider carefully what we think we should do in the circumstances.

How would you :

(a) Explain what you mean by "the seaside" to a schoolboy who has never seen the sea?

(b) Teach a little girl to ride a bicycle?

(c) Convince a friend that you can make a good omelet?

(d) Direct a stranger to a distant railway station?

(e) Describe how a penguin walks to some children who have never seen one?

These things may seem to have little to do with religious teaching, but they really can help us quite a lot, if we remember that teaching is not "giving a lesson", but sharing knowledge. For example, very much the same methods would be used in teaching a child to ride a bicycle, and teaching a child to pray. Learning to cycle and learning to pray are both acts of faith—the child must believe that it is possible before she can do either. And the teacher of either must know how to do it himself; be able to show her how to do it; arouse the child's faith that she can do it too; hold the child up; give her confidence, and encourage her to do it alone. The cycling instructor will also teach the child the rules of the road, and help her to develop a road sense. The teacher of prayer will teach the rules of the way of prayer, and help the child to develop a sense of spiritual things.

Again, we have to help the children to understand unseen things, and we shall use similar methods to those with which we describe the unknown things of this world.

So we see that teaching is not such a formal or unnatural thing as we may have imagined, but something that is partly made up of things like common sense, enthusiasm, and experience. But these are not by any means all that is necessary; they are like the threads stretched lengthwise on a loom, across which the coloured strands are woven to make the pattern. The various methods are like these coloured strands, and the many patterns they can make have to be carefully studied.

And it does not all rest with us. We are trying to give something to living people—not just pouring it into empty jars—and we have to get them to do their part. And for this three important things are needed. We could not even begin to teach any of the things suggested above unless the other people were interested and also gave us their attention, and what we taught would be of little use to them unless they remembered it. It is therefore of the utmost importance that the teacher of religion should understand these three things —*Interest*, *Attention*, and *Memory*, and know how they can be developed and used, before attempting the task of giving religious instruction to children.

CHAPTER 2

INTEREST

Before a child can express his own thoughts he has already learnt a great many things, and has quite a store of ideas and even opinions, and all this must be taken into account if we want to interest him, for he is much more likely to be interested in something connected with, or leading on from, what he already knows than in something entirely new and strange. So our first concern must be to discover what are the normal interests of children at the different stages of their growth and development. This is not very easy, because children not only differ very much in themselves, but their interests also depend to a great extent on their home conditions, and "the normal child" is almost as vague a term as "the man in the street". Yet it is possible, without making any hard-and-fast rules, to think of the children in age-groups and discover the kind of thing that mostly interests children at these ages.

The usual age-groups are : (1) from 2-5; (2) from 5-7; (3) from 7-11; and (4) the over 11's, often sub-divided into 11-13 and 13-15 or 16.

The first group is the age of the Nursery School, and we will consider first of all the things that are most likely to interest children from 2-5.

As their knowledge of life is mainly confined to the home, their interest will readily be given to anything connected with home life, They are still babies, being cared for and protected by grown-up people, and so they will be very

5

interested in other little, helpless things. They are at the very beginning of their voyage of discovery through life, and are continually adding to their store of knowledge by the use of their five senses of taste, touch, sight, hearing, and smell— at this age probably in this order. So they will be interested in things that they can examine in any of these ways, in order to find out what they are like. Having made their examination, they will sometimes ask : "What is it ?"

Here is an illustration of the strong interest which the *taste* of a thing has for children of this age—a very natural thing if we remember how the first impulse of an infant is to put things in his mouth.

A teacher was to give a lesson about an Eskimo baby to a small Nursery School. She prepared a snow village in a sand-tray, using salt instead of sand. She took infinite pains in making round, clay snow houses, tiny sledges with little woolly dogs harnessed to them, and small Eskimo people. She had looked forward to a delightful afternoon with the babies, playing with the snow village; but the children had no interest to spare for seeing, hearing, or handling, because they discovered at the outset the delight of digging their fingers into the "snow" and then sucking them.

Two fatal errors had been made on this occasion. It was a mistake to use anything so attractive as salt; and the toys were too small to interest children of this age. They need objects with a shape they can *feel* as well as see.

The second group, from the age of 5-7, is that of the Kindergarten. Nearly all children at this age go to a Day School, even if they have not been going before, and for them a new world is opening up outside the little home circle in which they have so far been living. They are meeting new people, and beginning to make friends. It is good to hear the small person of six refer, with great satis-faction, to "my friend". They are beginning to experience human relationships other than those of the family. So their interests will widen to include this larger world, and they will be interested in some of the things other people do, so long as they are simple and definite, and concerned with people rather than things.

Their main interest in *things* is for their use. They still ask, "What?" but a too literal answer will be met with an emphatic, "Yes, but what is it *for*?" If a child were to ask an adult, "What is a knife?" he might be told that it is a finely tempered steel blade, with a sharpened edge, and set into a handle of wood, horn, or ivory. If an adult put the same question to a child of this age the unhesitating answer would be, "To cut with". This is all that the child wants to know, and any more elaborate explanation will only bore him. It is true that he will probably ask the further question, "Why?" but his curiosity is not concerned with why the knife cuts, but rather with why an implement that cuts should be called by so odd a name as "knife", and not quite simply "a cutter"!

At this age life is becoming more adventurous, because the children are beginning to be allowed to go out alone, and have daily to journey through the exciting tract of No-man's-land between the two familiar worlds of home and school. Though they may still be too timid to venture far in exploring this unknown territory, they will be able to take an interest in other people's adventures.

This is also the age of delight in fairy stories, and the dividing line between the real world and fairyland is not at all clearly marked. In a world where every new discovery is wonderful, anything can happen and everything is possible. This is the age for laying the foundations of a living faith. We know that what we want to teach them is true, so we need feel no compunction about planting it in the hearts and minds of the children at the time when they can most readily accept and believe it. In later years of doubt these early lessons will stand them in good stead, and their influence should prove stronger than any temptation to fall away.

The child in the age-group 7-11 years is in what is often called the Junior School Department, and it will be convenient for our purpose to refer to him as the Junior Child.

It would probably be easier to give a list of the things in which the Junior Child is *not* interested than to cover the vast ground of the things in which he *is* interested! Normally, at this age, he is not interested in ideas, and his interest in people is for what they do rather than for what they are; and in things also for what they do rather than in how they do it. Though his most frequent question is probably, "Why?" it is a practical question requiring a practical answer. If he asks why his bicycle has to be oiled, he will be content with the answer that there are ball bearings in the hub that help the wheel to turn smoothly, and if they are not oiled they will rub against each other and get scratched. And although he may proceed to take off the wheel, it will be in order to see what the bearings are like, and not to study the mechanism of friction.

Apart from these distinctions, almost everything is of interest to the child of this age, and we can consider here only a few of the main lines of this interest.

Great changes are taking place in his home life, and he is no longer a person for whom everything has to be done. In fact, he is frequently being called upon to do things for other members of the family, and this gives him a new interest in the family as a unit. At this age children really do delight in doing things which to many grown-ups seem tiresome and boring. This may be because it is the *doing* that is the main interest, rather than the particular thing being done. For example, he is generally ready to run on an errand, though the errand itself may be the purchase of something for which he himself would have no use; it is the *something to do* which is the attraction. That is, something to do for some-one else, which is a new element in his life. So, in all the various home activities, there will be the persistent request, "Let me do that". A small child of 6 had been allowed to wash up the tea-things. On being told that there were no more to be done she washed them all over again, for the pure joy of doing it! A girl of 7 and her brother $8\frac{1}{2}$ elected, on their own initiative, to get breakfast each morning, their first task being to make their mother a cup of tea which one of them would take up to her. A girl of $8\frac{1}{2}$ wrote, "It is Mummy's birthday to-day. I made Mummy's birthday cake".

The school life of the Junior Child is also undergoing a change. He has "gone up" into a new department, often in an entirely different building. In his work there will be much less of the play element, but there will, or at any rate should, be much more in the way of organized games. He will gradually become interested in team games; in mastering the rules of the games; in seeing that everyone plays fair. Besides teams—which at this stage are not usually per-manent—there will be other things to join : Cubs, or Brownies, and various other groups, all appealing to his new sense of membership. Countless other interests are provided in most schools—nature-study, showing the many different ways in which things live and grow; competitions, many of them taking the form of collecting things, and so providing an interest in the things collected; school libraries, encouraging a taste for independent reading; radio and television, arousing interest in current events.

In the larger world he is coming into touch with many more people—shopkeepers, bus and tram conductors, as well as fellow-passengers and wayfarers. Some he will come to admire tremendously, generally because they are doing such delightful things. The child of this age will often have a curious assortment of friends in many different walks of life, to whose opinions he attaches very great importance. These may include the man who breaks up the road with a drill; the milkman, whom he will accompany on his rounds at the week-end; the school crossing patrol; the man who works the petrol pumps. Then there will be more remote heroes, such as a favourite film actor (not necessarily a star), or a local or international football player. Many of the characters from books will be real friends and companions.

A small boy of this age was taken by an aunt to visit a friend whose father was an alpine boot specialist. When they were about to leave, the boy whispered to his aunt, "Aren't we going to see Mr—?" At first she could not understand his request, as they had never met, but the next moment she remembered his interest in a recent Mount Everest expedition, and realized what a thrill it would be for the boy to shake hands with the man who had made the boots in which the mountaineers had climbed. So the introduction was made, to the mutual pleasure of both man and boy.

Lastly, there will be a new interest in himself, and his own increasing powers and abilities. This is possibly the outcome of his growing sense of importance in the three spheres of his life referred to above. He will begin to have very definite ideas as to what he wants to do when he grows up, and a simple faith in his ability to do it. Even now, through lack of experience of difficulties, he will often attempt to do things that an older person would know to be far beyond his own powers. For example, he will be quite sure that he can carry home from the railway station a suitcase which is too heavy for his mother; or that he can mend a broken chair-leg which his father knows will need a carpenter's skill. A little girl beginning to learn embroidery will confidently expect to be able to make a set of table mats at her first attempt.

A boy of 10, who had been visiting in the country with his mother and younger sister, begged his mother to promise that when they returned to their home in London she would let him go on ahead of them, by the early train, to get the house ready for them!

We must now consider the child in the last of our age-groups, from the age of 11 onwards. First we will think of him between the ages of 11 and 13 years. About this time the tendency for interests to widen is offset by an inclination to specialize. *Things* are now becoming much more interesting than *people*—in fact it sometimes seems that people hardly count at all except in so far as they provide the means and the opportunity for him to pursue his other interests. Heroes are only heroes so long as they achieve what is expected of them, and a very high standard is set.

In regard to things, the absorbing interest is now the answer to the question, "How?" He will take his bicycle to pieces in order to discover how it works, and, having done so, he will put it together again. This implies an interest in the mind that invented the mechanism, or at least in the *idea* that was behind the invention. So this older child is beginning to be interested in ideas, and can follow with interest a simple line of thought.

According to his special bent, he will be interested in travel, adventure, history, machinery, art, literature, music. One schoolboy of 12 suddenly presented his master with a carefully written account of the origin and history of each of the musical instruments in an orchestra. It had taken him months to compile, and no one had any idea that he was doing it!

Others are interested in scientific discoveries, chemistry, photography, etc.

Until now the interests of boys and girls have been much the same, but in this older age-group they begin to diverge and, on the whole, the girl will find a good deal to interest her in the home, while the boy will tend to regard the home mainly as his workshop. There is no hard-and-fast rule about this, and in some cases the position is reversed, but it is possible at this stage to consider separately some of the normal interests of the older boy or girl.

Both are interested in making things, but the things made by the girl are—usually—more domestic in character. She likes to shop, if the things to be bought interest her; and she enjoys knitting, sewing, and cooking, provided the things she makes are real and are going to be used. The boy may be more inclined to make things that are experimental and, therefore, less "useful".

The girl is more likely than the boy to be interested in babies and younger children. But an older boy will often be extremely good with the little ones. One boy of 12 who was conspicuous for bad behaviour in Sunday School, always brought his two little sisters to Evensong and sat with them in the front pew. Throughout the service he not only be- haved beautifully himself but, without any fuss, saw to it that the two little girls did so too.

The boy is usually more interested than the girl in the gang or group. While Guiding is often one of many interests for the girl, Scouting may absorb the whole interest of the boy, and his other pursuits be regarded as parts of his Scouting activities.

Children in the older part of this age-group, from the age of 13 to 15 or 16, are already entering adolescence—a diffi- cult time both for the children and for those who teach them. Their religious education should be in the hands of experts, and under the direction of the clergy.

New schemes for arousing, and holding, the interest of these older children have been thought out, and various types of organization are being tried, but they are still in the experimental stage. Every effort should be made to encourage these children to join in the normal family worship of their Parish Church on Sundays.

Very little need be said here about children over 13, since those who have not had special training should not be required to instruct them. Most of the tendencies that we have already noted with the 11-13-year-olds are accentuated. These children become more definitely specialists and may now embark upon hobbies that will hold their interest for the rest of their lives, such as boating, fishing, mountaineering, etc. Some are becoming interested in ideas, and are anxious to know both sides of a controversial subject. The relatives of a boy of about 16 were very troubled because his schoolmaster was reading to the boys, during the Scripture period, a book written by a non-Christian expressing heretical views. It was felt to be unnecessary, if not actually unwise, to introduce these boys to heresies before they were sufficiently established in the true doctrine of the Church to be able to see where they were wrong. The boy, who is now an ordained priest, has said that what first made him *think* about religion, and therefore become interested in it, was the reading of this heretical book!

There is a more marked difference in the interests of boys and girls at this age, and this tends to keep them apart until towards the end of the period, when they begin to be drawn together by their awakening mutual interest in each other.

At this age children usually have either a keen interest in games and sports, or none at all.

A convenient way of remembering these different age-group interests is to think of them in connection with the characteristic question of each group:

(a) The Nursery Child asks, "What?" (Meaning, "What is it?")

(b) The Kindergarten Child asks, "What?" (Meaning, "What is it for?")

(c) The Junior Child asks, "Why?"

(d) The Secondary Child asks, "How?"

One other word must be said about Interest. In some cases a child's interest in what we want him to learn will have to be deliberately aroused because, although actually there, it is *dormant*—that is, asleep—and has to be wakened. One of the main purposes in studying methods is to discover the most successful ways in which to arouse dormant interest in things that the children do not come across in the ordinary course of their life, but which we know to be of vital importance to them. The various ways in which this is done—by the use of pictures, objects of interest, music, etc.— will be considered later on when studying methods in relation to actual teaching, and it will be helpful when doing this to remember that there is this definite purpose in view.

It is a good plan to watch children of different ages, when this can be done without their realizing it, and to notice the things in which they each show interest. It can also be helpful to think back into our own childhood at some of these ages, and to try to remember the things that interested *us*.

Books in which the characters are children should be read, such as those by Noel Streatfeild. The first two sections of The Kenneth Grahame Book, *The Golden Age*, and *Dream Days*, would also be of interest to those who are studying children. Although the home life of the children described is not normal, the children themselves are very real, and their differing interests are clearly marked.

CHAPTER 3

ATTENTION

If we were content merely to interest the children in our care we should never succeed in teaching them anything. They would flit like butterflies from one interesting thing to another and, at the end, their minds would be a confused jumble. The whole purpose of understanding the interests of the children is to enable us to gain and hold their attention, so that we can go on to arouse their interest in the new thing that we want them to know.

Attention can be a very unreliable and unaccountable thing until we have come to understand its relation to Interest. A car would be a very unreliable thing to a driver who knew nothing about its petrol consumption, and his surprise when it suddenly stopped for want of petrol would be very like that of the uninstructed teacher who finds that the attention of a class has stopped for want of interest.

Interest is the feeling about a thing that makes attention to it possible, and it is quite literally impossible for a young child to give any attention at all to something that does not in the least interest him. This is what makes all that has already been said so necessary and important.

Having reached this point, we can now go on to consider the next stage. Interest is a feeling, attention is an activity and is, therefore, something which can be directed and used. It is of two kinds—*involuntary* (or, as it is sometimes called, *spontaneous*) and *voluntary*. The first is the kind that we mean when we say, "Something attracted my attention", and the second is referred to when we say, "I gave her my whole attention". The first is accidental and unintentional, and the second is deliberate, and an activity of the will. Both are the outcome of an interest, but the first interest is a passing one and the second an absorbing one.

Imagine that someone is reading a book which has not a very interesting beginning though the title has aroused his interest. Then there is a sound of hammering next door, and instantly, without any effort on his part, his attention is attracted and he begins to wonder what is being done. If, however, he makes an effort he can bring his attention back to the book and persevere with the reading. As he gets into the book it begins to grip him, and before long he is so deeply absorbed that he is no longer aware of the hammering next door.

This illustration shows us three ways of attending. To begin with the reader is *trying* to attend to the book, but cannot do so because it does not interest him; then he gives sudden, involuntary attention to the hammering; next he gives voluntary attention to the book, making a strong effort of the will; lastly, he is so interested in the book that his attention to it has become involuntary.

From this we can see that there are two kinds of involuntary attention : (a) passing and (b) sustained. The second is of much more value than the first, and even more valuable than voluntary attention since it requires no conscious effort and so does not tire, and one is able to understand, weigh up, and pass judgement on that which is holding one's attention, instead of using up all one's energy in attending to it.

It must, therefore, be the purpose of the teacher to lead the children from *passing involuntary attention* to *voluntary attention*, and then on to *sustained involuntary attention*, so that the lesson material may be not only learnt, but learnt understandingly.

But all children are not equally able to do this. The very young child is only able to give passing involuntary attention; but by the time the Nursery School age is reached it should be possible for the child to give voluntary attention for a few moments. If that does not pass on fairly quickly to the third stage, the effort to attend will be given up and the child's attention will wander off to something of greater interest.

This can be illustrated by the story already told of the snow village made of salt. The scene certainly attracted involuntary attention, and for a moment the voluntary attention of the children was held. But before it could become sustained and involuntary, their attention had been attracted by the salt. A few seconds' voluntary attention given to the fact that it was a pleasant thing to suck their fingers after handling it, resulted in their giving their whole and sustained involuntary attention to the delights of sucking salt fingers to the exclusion of all other interests.

The amount of sustained attention that a child at this age can give varies very much, according to the interest which accompanies it. For purposes of teaching it is well not to expect to hold it for more than five or six minutes on any one activity, that is, listening, watching, doing; by combining these activities, however, a young child's attention can be held for some considerable time.

The Kindergarten Child is capable of a slightly longer effort of will, and it is therefore possible to lead him more deliberately on to the third stage. He can also give sustained attention for a longer period and will listen to a story for ten or fifteen minutes, provided it is one he can understand and like, and it is well told.

One can hold both the voluntary and the sustained attention of the Junior Child for much longer periods, and it is a good thing to encourage the effort of will necessary for giving voluntary attention to something that is not immediately interesting. But at this age it must not be continued too long, and the third stage must be reached well before there are any signs of wandering attention.

The amount of sustained attention that can be held will depend very much on the subject, but it can often extend over two or three weeks, provided there are frequent opportunities for reviving it during that time.

In considering the kind and amount of attention which can be given by children over eleven, we have to bear in mind that various types of secondary education are provided in day schools : academic, technical, and practical. Because of this, the children tend to have different interests, and their methods of approach to the study of those interests is correspondingly different. Some will be able to give a considerable amount of voluntary attention to a subject not immediately interesting if it is the means to a desirable end, but it cannot be assumed that all will do so. Some form of competitive work is often useful in helping children to acquire necessary information, by their own efforts, even when it is outside their normal fields of interest. Sometimes it is possible to lead them, along the lines of their own interests, to discover new ones. Once interest in a subject has really been aroused, by whatever method, it can hold their sustained attention over a long period of time, often running into weeks and even months. This is of immense value in the teaching of these older children, who are capable of acquiring much more information on any subject than could possibly be given in one lesson period.

It is interesting to work out experiments with oneself to see if one can distinguish between these three kinds of attention, using such occasions as listening to the wireless news, seeing a cinema news reel, or reading a book in a room in which other people are talking; or to try experiments on other people to see how long it takes to attract their attention when they are occupied with something else. The results are often surprising.

CHAPTER 4

MEMORY

THERE are two kinds of memory. Some things make such a deep impression upon us that we never forget them. They are remembered without any effort and seem to have become a part of us. Other things we can only remember after much effort and frequent repetition. The first kind is called *simple memory* and the second kind *habit memory*. Most of our childhood memories are of the first kind, but as we grow older memorizing usually requires more and more effort. This is probably why people when they are old can remember their childhood so much better than later periods in their lives. When we are children everything is so new and wonderful that most things make a very strong impression. Later on, when our minds are packed with information and experiences it is much more difficult to get anything new into them.

If you tell a story to a young child, and then repeat it another day, he will tell you at once if you put in a different word. You will have to tell a story many times to an older child before he knew it well enough to do this.

But although the small child can remember a story that has been told to him once, he does not necessarily get the full meaning of it until he has heard it many times. Fortunately, he loves repetition and will listen to a favourite, oft-told story much more readily than to an untried new one. So it can be repeated again and again until not only the story, but also the truth we want it to teach, has been understood and learnt.

19

The little child can very quickly learn by heart from repetition, and will easily learn in this way a string of quite meaningless words, such as "Hey, diddle, diddle", "Dickery, dickery, dock", or "Fee, fi, fo, fum". So we have to be on our guard against taking it for granted that, because a small child can sing a particular hymn, or say a prayer, it means something to him.

As the child gets older it is easier for him to learn by heart if he understands the meaning of the words he is learning, while at the same time his capacity for memorizing steadily increases. It is, therefore, tremendously important that we should understand how to make use of this natural gift of childhood so that the child can have in his possession a store of poems, verses, prayers, and acts of praise which enshrine the truths of the Christian religion, as these not only give him words in which to express his faith, but will also help him to keep fast hold of that faith in times of doubt.

A girl of 15, who was going through a critical period in her spiritual life, was tremendously helped by a verse of a hymn with which she had become familiar in childhood, and which she repeated again and again at each temptation to doubt :

> I do believe, I will believe
> That Jesus died for me;
> That on the Cross he shed his Blood
> From sin to set me free.

Whenever we have remembered anything, three things have happened. The particular thing has found its way into our mind; our mind has been able to hold it; and we have been able to find it there when we wanted it. These three things are known as *Impression, Retention,* and *Recall.*

1. *Impression.* Unless the matter to be remembered made some sort of impression on our mind it would never gain admission to it, and the things most likely to make a deep

impression are those in which we are interested, or that are very closely related to our interests.

Some impressions are pleasant, others are unpleasant, and the particular kind of impression a thing first makes is likely to remain, unless some later experience brings about a change. That is to say, if the first impression is unpleasant we shall probably continue to dislike that thing for the rest of our lives, unless it gains, later on, a new and pleasing association. For instance, a child who has been frightened by a dog will probably always dislike dogs, unless he is helped to overcome the dislike, perhaps by being given a puppy of his own which he learns to love. When the puppy becomes a dog, his dislike for dogs in general will fade. So we must be very careful to see to it that the first impressions our children receive in their religious teaching are happy ones. Our knowledge of their interests at each stage of their development will help us to do this.

2. *Retention*. If the mind is to hold the matter that has been impressed upon it, the material must be suitable and presented in a form in which it can most easily be received. Quite a number of things make an impression on us, but they are not all retained in the mind, either because they do not appeal to us or because we do not understand them. So it is with children. It is not enough for them to be interested in the subject we are trying to teach them, we must present it to them in a form in which they can understand it. It is rather like the way that a mother bird feeds her young: she first eats and partly digests the food, and then gives it to the chicks who, although very interested in the food, could not digest it in its natural state. We often have to "pre-digest" our material before we present it to the children. If they are to enjoy it they must be able to understand it; if they do not understand it, it will not be retained.

There is another point to be considered. We have already noted that it is difficult to get new ideas into minds which are already packed with information and experiences; it is still more difficult to retain them. In fact, it is really only possible to retain new information if it is closely linked with knowledge and experiences gained throughout life. Facts not so linked tend to be forgotten. This process goes on all through life, and in time we do it more or less unconsciously. But children need to be helped, and a good teacher will be careful to see that no new material is presented to a child without carefully linking it up with what is already known.

For example, if one were to tell a story about a swan to children who had neither seen nor heard of one before, and had no idea what kind of creature it is, they would probably have forgotten everything about it by the time they reached home, even if they took any of it in at all. But if the children were first allowed to talk about birds with which they were familiar, and especially any that swim, and to discuss their different sizes and colours, then the new idea of a swan could be linked to these by pointing out both the resemblances and the differences, and the children would be able to add to their existing knowledge of birds the new information about swans.

A useful rule to remind us of the need to link up new material with old is, "Always lead from the known to the unknown."

3. *Recall.* If we were actively remembering, all the time, everything that our minds retained we should either be in a continual state of bewilderment, or we should have to limit very drastically the number of things we let into our minds. Fortunately this is not necessary, for our minds are so made that we can store things up in them. They are rather like a library with rows of shelves filled with books. The owner of a library would not remember exactly what was in every book on his shelves, but he would know where to find what he wanted when he needed it. This is how our minds should be, and can be if we train them properly. If we can learn to

pack away all our bits of knowledge alongside other items of the same kind, we shall know which "shelf" to go to whenever we need to recall that knowledge. The mind must put things away somewhere, and it rests with ourselves how this is done. It is the disorderly mind, which stows things away just anywhere, that cannot remember. It is important to understand this so that we can help the children to link up all new information with some similar knowledge already in their minds, so that it will be put away tidily on the proper shelf and be ready to hand whenever needed.

But the books on the shelf need looking after—dusting and airing, and sometimes re-arranging. And, of course, they are there to be read. So we must provide opportunities for the children to dust their shelves from time to time, and to read and re-read the books upon them. This is what we mean by *revision*. By means of frequent revision we are helping the children to practise finding quickly what they want, and to learn their way about their own minds, which is just as important as learning to keep them tidy.

Later on we shall see how all these things fit into the various methods in teaching, but there is one point that should be considered here, and that is the best method to be used when we want children to learn something by heart. We have seen that it is easier for a child to remember something which he both likes and understands, but also that it is possible for him to get by heart something quite meaningless —and he can do this even when it is distasteful, if there is sufficient inducement. In the teaching of religion this form of learning is neither desirable nor necessary, and we should see that the meaning of what is to be learnt is clear. In this we are helped by the fact that all knowledge comes to us through our senses, and so we are not dependent upon only one method of memorizing. There are two kinds of memory that can be employed for all general purposes, and which should be very closely associated. They are *Oral Memory*, which depends on the power to remember what has been heard, and *Visual Memory*, which depends on the power to remember what has been seen. Most people have both these two kinds of memory, but one of them is generally stronger than the other. With children both should be used together, especially when dealing with *ideas*. For example, before teaching the words of the hymn *All things bright and beautiful*, there should be a talk describing beautiful scenery, perhaps in the form of taking the children for an imaginary walk in the country; and pictures of birds, flowers, rivers, and mountains should be shown. The words to be learnt will then be filled with meaning and there will be no difficulty about committing them to memory.

Again, before teaching the Twenty-third Psalm, a word-picture of the life of an eastern shepherd should be given, and also pictures or models of the things that he uses—such as the sling, the rod, and the staff—shown.

If we are teaching a hymn or a poem, we can see at once that no one line of it, by itself, can be either pleasing or intelligible to a child, and so it is clear that the old method of learning line by line is not a good one. It will be found that children will learn a verse much more quickly *as a whole* than they will by constant repetition of one line at a time.

We can test this by experimenting with ourselves : choose two short poems of equal length and note how long it takes to learn one of them line by line, and the other by reading it straight through until it is known. Then take two others that you have read before, one of which you like and one you dislike, and compare the time it takes to learn each of them by heart.

CHAPTER 5

WE have been thinking a little about the teacher, and a good deal about the children to be taught. Now we must consider what we are going to teach. This all comes under the heading of *Purpose*, and we must be quite sure what our purpose is before we can start making our *Plan* for carrying it out.

Put into general terms, we want to teach the children in our care about God, and his purpose for mankind, in such a way that they will learn to know him, to love him and to desire to serve and obey him. This covers a very wide range, and includes all that we can tell them about the Three Persons in the Blessed Trinity, as summarized in the Catechism, *God the Father, who hath made me, and all the world . . . God the Son, who hath redeemed me, and all mankind . . . God the Holy Ghost, who sanctifieth me, and all the elect people of God*; all that we can tell them about the Holy Catholic Church, both as an outward, visible fellowship of Christian people, and also as the mystical Body of Christ; all that this means for them as being members of this Body. We shall want to train them in prayer and worship, and to lead them in the way of righteousness, until religion for them becomes a true and living thing—not only a Faith which they hold, but one that holds them.

What a tremendous undertaking! How can we ever hope to accomplish it? Not in our own strength, certainly, and not all at once. That is one of the most common mistakes made by those who are beginning to teach : they realize that there is so much to be taught and try to teach too much at once. But there is no need for panic, we are only expected to set the children in the right direction, and to lead them along the first stages of a journey that will last through life. And we have all the years of their childhood in which to do it. It may be that a particular child will only be in our care for a short time : then we are only responsible for that time and must be content to meet the needs of the moment, and to trust that others will deal with later needs as they arise.

We can, however, make out a rough syllabus of the most suitable subjects to be taught to children at each stage of their development, according to the interests, and ability to attend, which we have already studied.

The very small children, of Nursery School age, are still being taken care of by grown-ups and the older children. They are very much aware of their need of protection, and want to feel safe. A child of this age will often run quite suddenly to his mother and want to be picked up, and then almost at once wriggle down again. He needs to be reassured that the place of refuge is still there, and although he is very happy playing by himself for quite long periods of time, he *must* hear someone moving about, doing things, within easy reach. If there is a sudden silence the child will probably call out, "Mummy, are you there?" or come running to make sure that his mother *is* there, and that he is safe.

We can therefore teach these little ones about the loving heavenly Father who takes care of all little, helpless things. This can be done in many ways : through nature stories about flowers and trees, and the care that is taken of the little buds; about birds, and their nests and eggs, and the little baby chicks; about many different kinds of animals, and the ways in which they care for their young; and about all kinds of children, including children of far-away lands who have never heard about the heavenly Father.

In a course of Nature Lessons to a Sunday Nursery School on God's care for his creatures, one lesson was given on *The Snail*, and snails were taken along for the children to see, and touch, the little houses God had given them to wear on their backs, because they could not run fast enough to get home safely, if they had to leave their houses behind. Simple lessons could be given about the polar bear, and other animals which live in snowy countries, and have white coats to match; about peas or other seeds that grow in pods to keep them safe; about kangaroos and wallabies, who have warm pockets in which to carry their babies; about daffodils and the little sheath that covers the bud, like a warm blanket, until the flower is ready to open; about people who live in hot countries and have dark skins so that the sun will not burn them. Stories can be told of the different ways in which mothers in far-away lands look after their little ones—the Esquimo who puts her baby in the snow to keep it warm, and the Red Indian who carries hers on her back in a bag stuffed with soft moss.

There are a few Bible stories about babies and children, e.g. Baby Moses, the birth of John the Baptist, Jesus blessing the children. The stories of the Baby Jesus should be given a very special place, and need not be reserved only for Christmas time, because times and seasons mean nothing at this age, and a year is a very long time for the children to wait to hear the stories again.

The stories should not all be about other people, for we want the children to realize God's love and care for *them*. So we shall make stories for them about their own homes, and their food and clothes. Nor need they all be about children, for the heavenly Father cares for grown-up people as well, and unless the children realize this they may become fearful of growing up. We must help them to realize that we are all one Family, and that God is the loving Father of all.

This does not mean that we can only teach about God taking care of us; but this should be our main theme, and the background of all our teaching with the Nursery Child. For example, we might have a lesson on flowers in which we did not mention God at all; but at the end a strong suggestion would be made by saying, "Shall we say 'Thank you' to our Father in heaven for making these flowers so lovely?"

In the Kindergarten the children are learning to make friends, both with other children and with their grown-up teachers. So this is a good time to teach about Jesus, the Friend of little children, and also the Friend of all kind and happy people, as well as of those who are sick and sad. If the Gospel stories are told now they will never be forgotten, and the children will not tire of hearing them. There will also be stories about the friends of Jesus, and what they did after he had gone back to the heavenly Father so that he could help them better. Many stories of later Saints are also suitable for these young children.

Missionary stories will appeal to the dawning spirit of adventure, as well as telling about yet more friends of Jesus. Many of these stories have elements which appeal to the same sense of wonder that delights in fairy tales, and are of permanent value because they will not have to be "un-believed-in" later on. And we must not forget the friends of Jesus who are also friends of the children—the clergy of the parish, doctors, nurses, teachers, etc.

Remembering the favourite question, "What is it for?" we can now teach the children about their Parish Church, the place where the friends of God meet together to offer him their love and praise and thanks; the uses of the different parts of the Church can be explained—the Font, where the Friend of little children takes them in his arms to bless them and make them his own; the big Bible, in which are to be found the stories of Jesus and his friends, and the Lectern, from which they are read; the Altar, where Jesus meets his friends in a very special way; the pulpit, where the Rector (or Vicar) stands to teach us about God. Every attempt should be made to make the children realize that the church, which is their heavenly Father's House, is their home because they are his children, members of his family, and friends of his beloved Son, Jesus Christ.

As with the younger children, this does not mean that all our lessons must be about Friends. But the idea of loving relationships, with God and with one another, should be the general theme, and prepare the way for fuller teaching on our duty to God and our duty to our neighbour, to be given later on.

Nor does it mean that we shall only teach about God the Father to the little ones, and only about God the Son to the children in the Kindergarten. To both we shall speak quite simply and naturally about God—Father, Son, and Holy Spirit— but the emphasis with the Nursery Child will be on the loving heavenly Father, and with the Kindergarten Child on Jesus Christ, the children's Friend, while later on the emphasis will be on the Person and work of the Holy Spirit. This is in line with God's own method in revealing himself to mankind; as Father first of all, then in the Person of Jesus Christ as the only-begotten Son of the Father, and finally in the Person of the Holy Spirit, coming from the Father and the Son. And it is in this same way that each one of us can best come to know God.

From our study of the normal interests of the Junior Child we can see that he is now ready to learn all the facts we can teach him about the great Society of which he is a member—the Holy Catholic Church. We must remember that it will be the people who make it up, and the things that it does, that will interest him, and not our thoughts and ideas about it. But these things will give us a large range of material for our lessons.

His new interest in himself and his own part in the various activities of life will enable him to appreciate the fact of his membership, with its privileges and responsibilities, and so it is very important to teach him about his Baptism, and to help him to understand something of what it means to be a member of Christ, the child of God, and an inheritor of the Kingdom of Heaven, and also to explain the meaning of the Baptismal promises.

This will include lessons about the Church as a Society : the members of the Society—that is, all baptized persons; the appointed ministers of the Church, why they wear robes and vestments, why they have special names, why they do the things that they do in church; the Church's Library—the books of the Bible, in which we learn about God and all that he has done for us, and the Prayer Book Services, in which we offer ourselves and our praises to God. Because of their growing sense of membership, the children of this age group can enter into the spirit of corporate worship if it is put to them as an opportunity for doing something for God, for each other, and for doing it together.

Their delight in doing things for other people can be used by suggesting ways of, and providing opportunities for, service within the fellowship of the Church. There is often a reluctance to let the Junior Child do things, from a mistaken anxiety that he will not do them well enough to be offered to God. Against this we can remember our Lord's acceptance of a boy's *five loaves and two small fishes*, and contrast his use of them with Andrew's *"What are these among so many?"*

There are quite a number of things that Junior children could do, if they were allowed to do them, and they can be of real service. They can help with the usual Saturday cleaning of the Church—dusting, throwing away the dead flowers, filling the vases with fresh water. Sometimes they could arrange some of the flowers. They could change the book-marks when the Church colours are changed. Some children are very good at polishing brass. Older ones can help with mending hassocks, etc. If a churchyard is no longer used as a burial-ground, it often has a neglected look; a band of youngsters, under supervision, could soon alter this by sweeping up dead leaves and tending any flowers that may be growing there. In parishes where there is a Family Eucharist followed by breakfast, the children love to take their turn at laying the tables and handing round the food. They can also be given notices to take round when the parish is being circularized.

Opportunities for service of this kind will help these children to feel that they belong to the Family, and that they are being of use, just as they are beginning to feel their usefulness in their own families at home. It might be found that children who were allowed to help, at an age when the desire to help is strong, would take more kindly, later on, to the idea of giving some of their time to the service of their parish church, as members of organizations for older children and young people. If a number of children wanted to help in some of these ways it would be necessary for them to take turns. It should always be regarded as a privilege, to be withdrawn from any child who persistently misused it.

Then there are the Rules of the Society, and these will require lessons on Prayer and the Sacraments, the Commandments, the Creed, and the Lord's Prayer. These can all be taught in a practical way if we think of it as learning to play the game of Christianity. All games have rules, and the players must know and keep them.

Although the Junior Child has not a very strong historical sense, he will be able to enjoy the thrilling stories of the early days of the Church, as well as countless others from her history all down the ages. And our own day must not be neglected—the work of the Church overseas provides stories every bit as enthralling as those of earlier times.

But chiefly we shall tell him about the great Founder of the Society which he has joined : his choosing and training the first leaders; the example he set his followers all through his life; his promise to be with us always, all through *our* lives.

Lastly, we can help the child to find not only many of his heroes, but also his friends, in the Society's Roll of Honour, the Saints of the Church, and the faithful servants of God in Old Testament times. Here there must be a word of warning. Much of the Old Testament can only rightly be understood in the light of our Lord's teaching about God and his purpose for men. There are many Old Testament stories which, apart from this fuller knowledge, give a wrong impression about the ways of God's workings with men. All such stories should be avoided until children have reached the age when they can exercise their judgement and learn to discern the truths embedded in the ancient setting of the Old Testament; truths which, because of the lack of fuller knowledge, were only part of the whole truth which our Lord Jesus Christ came to teach, but which prepared the minds of men to receive that teaching when, in the fulness of time, it was given.

Such stories as the Plagues of Egypt, or Samuel slaying Agag, should not be used. They do appeal to children, who have no experience of horror themselves and can, therefore, enjoy the vivid descriptions, and for this reason they are especially dangerous because they will make a very strong and lasting impression. It will be very difficult indeed to erase this impression in later years and the children will, therefore, build up their belief in God on a fundamentally wrong conception.

In the Nursery School and Kindergarten the Old Testament should hardly be used at all. The story of the finding of the baby Moses; of Hannah going to see her little boy, Samuel, and taking him the coat she had made; of David, the Shepherd Boy who became a King and served God; these could be taught from the point of view of God's loving care, and with the little ones we should not go beyond these.

But for Juniors many of the Old Testament stories are excellent, they are vivid and dramatic, and tell of men who put God and his will first in their lives, and set examples of noble character. For instance, Abraham is the great example of unquestioning faith and obedience; Joseph gives an example of a youth who firmly resisted temptation by putting his whole trust in God, even though it brought him suffering.

The Old Testament was the Bible of our Lord Jesus Christ and those he taught, and children can appreciate the fact that they are learning what he learnt as a Boy at school.

Stories of Saints give us similar examples of courage and faithfulness, and are suitable for children of all ages.

There is really very little that we cannot bring into our syllabus for the Junior Child, so long as we remember that we must keep to facts. This does not mean that we may not teach any doctrine at all. The Apostles' Creed is the Church's official statement of her Faith, yet each clause states a definite fact. So we can teach the facts on which these clauses are based, and we can encourage the child to learn each clause by heart. As we have already seen, the child can learn very easily by heart, and things learnt at this age are rarely entirely forgotten. If, therefore, the facts are learnt in this way and then committed to memory in a suitable form, they can be recalled at a later time and filled with deeper meaning as the child is able to receive it. In addition to all the other subject-matter suggested above, we shall teach suitable hymns and poems, verses from the Psalms, and the great Christian Acts of Praise, as well as some simple prayers. It will not always be possible to explain every word of these, but if the words are beautiful they will have a value of their own for the child, and he can add fuller meaning as he grows older. These could all be collected into a stout notebook, and illustrated.

The Secondary School Child is getting near the age for Confirmation, and in many cases the suggestion that he might like to be confirmed is sprung on him a week or two before the classes are starting. Often he has only a very vague idea as to what it all means, and he is advised to come to the classes in order to find out.

How very much better it would be if he were properly instructed long before the moment for decision came, and also filled with a desire to take this important step into full enjoyment of the privileges of membership, so that we had the child asking us when he could be confirmed, instead of our having to coax him to come to the class. This can be done, and it should be begun as soon as possible; and as the child is to be prepared for receiving the personal gift of the Holy Spirit, we shall spend the time at our disposal in teaching what we can about the work of God the Holy Spirit in the Church and in the lives of individual members.

This teaching will fit in very well with the interests of the child at this age. His keen interest in how things are done will encourage him to try to find out how it is that the Church has been able to live through all the terrible periods of persecution, heresy, unfaithfulness, and indifference that have so often threatened her with destruction; how it is that she has been able to keep her ministry unbroken, to administer her sacraments without failing, to guard her scriptures and her creeds from those who would have destroyed them. In all this the child can be led to see the working of God the Holy Spirit.

And again, in the lives of the individual members of the Church down the ages, he can recognize a power far beyond that of mere human strength. In the stories of saints and martyrs he will see the Holy Spirit at work, guiding, strengthening, and leading into all truth. From that he can go on to study the truth that has been revealed to the Church, through her sacred writings and also through the long succession of teachers who have been filled with the Holy Spirit.

The child over eleven is able to follow out simple reasoning and a clear line of thought, and so a fair amount of definite doctrine can be taught at this age. The Catechism forms an excellent syllabus, and can very usefully be learnt by heart, but it is equally necessary that it should be understood. It is possible to give simple instruction on the redemptive work of our Lord, with its meaning for us in the forgiveness of sins and the hope of eternal life; and our response of repentance, faith, and love, made in the power of the Holy Spirit.

But in studying the work of the Holy Spirit we need not be restricted to the Church. The Holy Spirit is manifested in everything that is good, true, beautiful. So we can allow the child to follow his own particular line of interest and find in it evidence of inspiration. We can help him to discover this in literature, art, music, architecture, medicine, science, and mechanics, and the more we can bring his normal interests into the sphere of the activity of the Holy Spirit, the more we can hope to make his religion a living reality to him.

If we now look back over our suggestions as to what to teach, we shall see that we have covered the ground of all the *things which a Christian ought to know and believe to his soul's health*, which is part of the charge given to Godparents when a child is baptized. This does not mean that by the time a child has been confirmed he should know everything that he will ever need to know—that never happens to anyone in this life. But he should by now have a good working knowledge of what it means to be a Christian, and how he can find grace and strength to play his part faithfully as a member of the Holy Catholic Church; as well as a real desire to learn more.

A Scheme of Training for Church Children, published by The Church Information Board, Church House, Westminster, S.W.1, sets out clearly the subject matter which children should be taught, and gives suggestions for things which children should know and do at certain stages of their development. In order that the children themselves may understand the importance of knowing and doing, *Achievement Cards* for Kindergarten, Junior, and Secondary children have been produced. These are of real interest to the children, and of assistance to teachers in their individual care of children.

CHAPTER 6

HOW TO PREPARE A LESSON FOR CLASS TEACHING

THOSE who give class teaching should know how to prepare a lesson. Many parishes provide some form of preparation class for those who are engaged in the work of religious education, both for the help and encouragement of the teachers, and also to ensure a systematic method in the teaching so that the right kind of instruction is given in each of the many departments, according to the age and capacity of the children. And where such classes are provided it should be a strictly enforced rule that those who do not attend the class may not teach.

But even so, there is room for a good deal of individual work in any teaching scheme, and each teacher must prepare his or her own lesson and bring it into its final stage to meet the requirements of the particular children to be taught.

Even at the class it will not be possible to discuss a lesson intelligently unless the teachers understand what a lesson should be like, and what are the different stages in it, and why they are so arranged. And so, whether there is a class or not, it is equally important for every teacher to learn how to prepare notes for the lesson he is going to teach.

The first stage in our lesson preparation is to decide what is to be our aim. We can see at once that we must have an aim—that is, some particular thing that we propose to have accomplished at the end of the lesson, otherwise we might as well spend the lesson time reading story-books. We have our general aim—to teach the children about our holy faith, and to help them to put the teaching into practice. But we cannot do all this in one lesson; it has to be spread over a period of years, and in each lesson we must be content to teach one point, and only one. Thus in each lesson there will be an intention to teach one thing, and that one thing is called the AIM of the lesson.

As the AIM refers to one thing only, it must be quite simple and definite, so that one can see at a glance what the lesson is intended to teach. As the intention is *To do* some particular thing, the AIM, when written down, will begin with the word *To*. Thus our AIM might be "To teach the great truth that God is Love", or "To show how a blind man was made happy", or "To help the children to understand why we say 'For Jesus Christ's sake' at the end of some of our prayers".

These three AIMS are all quite simple and direct, but they are not all equally easy. It is very important that the AIMS of our lessons should be suited to the needs and abilities of the children being taught, and they will therefore be easy for the little ones, and will increase in difficulty as the children grow older. Whether difficult, or easy, there must be only *one* point in each AIM, and a good rule to make is that the word *and* must never occur in an AIM. So we can say our AIM is "To teach that God is love", *or* "To show how God helps us when we are in trouble"; but we must *not* say "To teach that God is love and that he helps us when we are in trouble". There is good reason for this: if we try to teach two things at once, we shall find that something we want to say does not fit both, so we shall leave it out, only to realize later on that our lesson does not hold together without it; and we shall end up by confusing the children completely, and not teaching them either of the two points. But if we are patient, and content to teach one thing at a time, we shall find that each lesson can be properly taught and something definite accomplished.

Along with the AIM we have to choose our LESSON
SUBJECT, and sometimes one will be chosen first, sometimes
the other. For example, with the first of the three AIMS
mentioned above we should choose it first and then decide
what story would best teach this great truth to the children.
We might use the story that our Lord used, the Prodigal
Son, and we should then begin our Lesson Notes like this:

SUBJECT: The Story of the Prodigal Son.

AIM: To teach the great truth that God is Love.

But with the second AIM we could begin with the intention
of giving a lesson about Blind Bartimæus, and our second
step will then be to decide what our AIM is to be. The
story can be told from the point of view of our Lord, or of
Bartimæus, or even of the crowd that thronged Jesus, and
in each case our AIM would be slightly different. Our
choice would depend on the age of the children—the first
for the very little ones who like to hear of people being
cared for; the second for rather older ones, about 5 or 6,
who are becoming interested in individuals and will like
to know more about what Bartimæus did; and the third
for bigger children of 7 or 8 who know the story quite
well, and will enjoy thinking about it from an entirely
new angle. The AIM suggested above is obviously for the
second of these, and the Lesson Notes would start like
this:

SUBJECT: The Healing of Blind Bartimæus.

AIM: To show how a blind man was made happy.

Next we have to think out what APPARATUS we shall
need for the particular lesson we are going to give. This
includes what we shall use ourselves and also what the
children may like to use. There is a wide range of choice,
and we should be careful not to use so much that the
children are confused. It is unwise, with little ones, to do
a blackboard drawing *and* to show a picture of the same
thing, though a model and a picture can be helpful if they

both look similar—as, for example, a model and a picture of an eastern house. If the children are going to use sand-trays they will not need paper and pencils for drawing as well, though they could sometimes be given a choice when the lesson is a suitable one.

For the lesson on Blind Bartimæus a blackboard and coloured chalks, and a model of an eastern house, could be used by the teacher; paper, crayons, and cutting-out scissors by the children. The APPARATUS must be added to our Lesson Notes.

We now have to consider the Biblical References, and first of all we must decide from which Gospel we shall take the story. In some ways Luke's account is the best one for our purpose : it tells of the questioning by Bartimæus when he heard the multitude, and the answer given him; it gives our Lord's words, *Receive thy sight*; and it tells of Bartimæus glorifying God, and the people giving praise unto God. On the other hand, Luke does not give the blind man's name, which is only mentioned in Mark's account, where we are also given rather more detail about the way in which Bartimæus received the news, *he calleth thee*. It would therefore be a good plan to read the two accounts and make the fullest use of both. There is a difficulty about doing this because, according to Luke's account, Jesus and his disciples were *entering* Jericho; Mark's account describes them as *leaving* it, apparently after passing through it. We must make our choice and be clear in our own mind which account we shall follow, but it is not necessary to say which way they were going unless the children ask. Then we must give a definite answer, according to the choice we have already made.

The multitudes probably consisted of fellow-pilgrims, all on their way to Jerusalem for the Feast of the Passover.

Under the AIM, in our lesson notes, we shall now put :

APPARATUS : Blackboard and coloured chalks; model of

an eastern house; paper, crayons, and cutting-out scissors.

BIBLICAL REFERENCES : Mark 10. 46-52; Luke 18. 35-43.

The Biblical References are very important, and we must also be careful to put the actual verses into our lesson notes at the places where we are going to use them. One reason for this is that we are often very much tempted to take liberties with the Bible stories, and to put into them things of our own imaginings in order to fill out the story. Another reason is that we are liable to think we know a story so well that we do not need to look it up. This may result in our leaving out an important point or, which may be far worse, putting in something which really belongs to another story! Quite experienced teachers have been known to do this. They know so many stories well, yet they can easily get them confused and put a detail from one episode into an entirely different one. When this is pointed out they sometimes say, "Do you know, I quite thought that bit came into this story"! It may be that the person from whom they first heard it failed to look the story up to make sure the details were correct. If we have the passage in the Bible constantly before us while we are preparing the lesson, we shall be able to check these tendencies; and the references in our notes will bring us back to the Bible at each stage of the lesson when we are going over it again for practice.

It has been said that it is the function of the Church to teach, and of the Bible to prove, and teachers of religion would do well to remember this. Whatever the age of the children, whenever we are giving a lesson from the Bible or making use of Biblical references in any way, we should as far as possible use the actual words. They are so very beautiful : the English of the Bible is the most lovely that has ever been written; the descriptions are so vivid and yet restrained; and though it often speaks of the most intimate things, there is a wonderful reserve in the language used. Even when the language is difficult, the children should be given the *real* Bible story although it will be necessary to put some of it into more simple words. This should be followed by quoting or reading a short passage from the Bible. For example, after describing the healing of Bartimæus, the actual words from the Bible should be read or quoted.

Older children should be encouraged to use and read the Bible whenever possible, so that they can become familiar with the language and style, as well as with its teaching, and also that they may learn to find their way about the Bible and so be able to use it intelligently.

Now we must get down to the lesson itself. Our notes will be for our own guidance, and not word for word what we are going to say to the children. What we have considered so far concerns our preparations for the lesson; what follows will be notes to help us to present our lesson to the children so that they will be able to follow and understand it. The notes must include all the important points, but only in the form of headings which we can get more or less by heart. When we have got on paper *what* we are going to say, we can go on to practise *how* we are going to say it, but it should not be necessary to write all that down.

Our lesson will contain new material and, as we have seen, this will have to be very carefully linked up with something which the children already know. In other words, we must *introduce* our subject to the children, and the part of the lesson in which we do this is called the INTRODUCTION. There are many ways of introducing a new lesson : if it is one of a course it is often a good plan to revise the previous lesson by asking a few questions about it, in order to get the right set of ideas into the children's minds ready for linking them up with the new ones. Sometimes we can show the children a familiar picture, and let them say what they remember about it. We can then perhaps draw their attention to something in it that has not been noticed before, and so lead on from that to the new material. We could let them look at a well-known hymn, and ask them if they know what a particular word or verse means, and then make the explanation form the first part of the lesson.

It must be borne in mind that the INTRODUCTION is not a part of the lesson, and that it must not contain any new material. It will be quite short, its purpose being to get the children thinking about the things with which the lesson subject can be associated.

With this particular lesson we could suggest their looking about the room and naming some of the things they can see; then they would all shut their eyes and realize that without them they would not be able to see any of these things. This could lead to questions as to whether they know anyone who cannot see, and so to a story about a man who was blind.

The children are now ready to have the lesson itself presented to them, and we call this the PRESENTATION stage. Here we have two things to work out : what we are to teach, and how we are to teach it. These are called Subject Matter, and Method. There are different ways of setting out the Presentation Stage of a lesson, and some teachers find one way more helpful, some another. Those who use a lesson book would probably find it best to follow the plan of the book, using the same headings but putting quite short notes under each, showing the points which are to be made and the methods to be used in making them. Normally there should not be more than three main headings, though each might have two or three sub-headings. Headings should be short and clear, and closely related, so that they provide a summary of the whole lesson.

Another plan, which is useful when lesson notes are being dictated, is to rule two columns and to head the left-hand one, which should be the smaller, Subject Matter, or

Summary because, when the column is finished, we should be able to read down it a summary of the whole lesson. The right-hand column will be headed, Method. Underneath the first heading we shall put, in order, all the main points with which we intend to deal; under the second heading, and opposite the various points, we shall write down the way in which we shall make each point, together with any Bible references.

When we have finished the lesson we shall want to round it off; and also to see what sort of impression it has made, by asking one or two questions about it. This rounding-off stage is called the CONCLUSION because it concludes the lesson. Sometimes it can be a short story which draws special attention to the chief point of the lesson; or it could take the form of looking at pictures that throw further light on what has been said. If questions are asked, they can either be about the lesson, to see if the children can remember it rightly, or they can be put in such a way that the children will have to think a little beyond what we have actually told them and so discover for themselves what we want the lesson to teach them. Another way is to let the children find a hymn that just fits, and discuss its bearing on the lesson.

There is still something left for us to do. We have noticed how much children like to be doing things, and we can satisfy this desire to *do* something, and at the same time give ourselves an opportunity to discover what impression our lesson has made and, if it is a wrong one, to put it right. The best way to do this is to let the children go over the main points of the lesson again, in their own minds, and either write some part of it down; draw something connected with it; or write an answer to some question about it. This part of the lesson comes under the heading, *Activity*, or *Things to do*. We must always be careful to see that what the children do is really their own activity, and not merely something that we have suggested. There is often a temptation to put our own thoughts into the children's minds at this stage, and get them to write what we want them to say. But this is of no value to them at all. If the work is not entirely their own self-expression it should not be attempted.

One other point should be borne in mind about the children's own activities. It is convenient to suggest the various things to do at the end of our lesson notes, but in many cases, especially with older children, the activities would more often be carried out throughout the lesson. Thus, in the making of a summary, as each point is made the children would write it down, either in their own words or by copying it from the blackboard, where it has been written from their own suggestions. A hymn would be looked up at the point where it fits; answers to questions could be written down, and compared, at the end of each section of the Presentation.

The following are notes for the lesson suggested above:

SUBJECT: The Healing of Blind Bartimæus (for children aged 6).

AIM: To show how a blind man was made happy.

APPARATUS: Blackboard and coloured chalks; model of an eastern house; paper, crayons, and cutting-out scissors.

BIBLICAL REFERENCES: Mark 10. 46-52; Luke 18. 35-43.

INTRODUCTION: Ask the children to look round the room and to name some of the pretty things they can see. Tell them to shut their eyes, and help them to realize that it is with their eyes that they are able to see the things they have named. Tell them that sometimes people are not able to see with their eyes and ask if they know anyone like that. What do we call them? How do they manage to walk about the streets? What work could they learn to do? Our story to-day is about a blind man who lived a long, long time ago.

PRESENTATION

1. THE BLIND MAN'S DAILY LIFE

(a) *His Home.* Tell his name and let children repeat it. Show model house. Describe city wall and gate. (Draw on blackboard.) Tell how he left home each morning and went out through gate, perhaps feeling his way with a stick.

(b) *His Begging.* Describe. Suggest he may have sat under a palm tree. (Draw him sitting there.) Picture him listening to sounds around him, and describe them (with actions where possible): people's footsteps, trotting donkeys, padding camels; voices of people gossiping and telling him news; the sound of money dropping into his bowl.

(c) *His Return Home.* At end of day he counts his few pennies and taps his way home. (Rub figure from blackboard.)

2. THE BLIND BEGGAR HEARS ABOUT JESUS

(a) *He sits near the Gate.* Describe, as before, his leaving home and sitting outside the gate. (Put him back in sketch on blackboard.) Imitate again the different sounds he heard.

(b) *He hears a new sound.* Describe: lots of footsteps, excited voices, the kind of noise made by a great crowd. Ask children if they can remember the noise made by a crowd. (Draw crowd on blackboard.)

(c) *He cries for help.* Tell of his question, "What does it mean?", and that his friends answer, *Jesus of Nazareth passeth by.* (Luke 18. 36, 37.) Bartimæus had heard about Jesus and knew he had healed people who were ill, and made blind people see. Jesus could make him see, if only he could get to him. Give his cry for help in direct speech. (Verse 38. Omit *Thou son of David.*)

3. THE BLIND MAN SEES JESUS

  (a) *He is told to be quiet.* People in the crowd hear his
      cry. They do not want to be stopped. They tell him
      to be quiet. He takes no notice but keeps on crying
      out, *Have mercy on me.* (Verse 39.)

  (b) *He is helped by his friends.* Someone else hears Barti-
      mæus. Someone who does not mind stopping. *Jesus
      stood still, and said, Call ye him.* His friends tell him
      it is all right, Jesus has heard him : *Be of good cheer:
      rise, he calleth thee.* They help him up; he throws off
      cloak that was wrapped round him and goes to Jesus.
      (Mark 10. 49, 50.)

  (c) *He is healed by Jesus.* Give question asked by Jesus,
      and answer of Bartimæus, in words of Bible. (Luke
      18. 41.) Pause before giving words of healing. Every-
      one in crowd waiting—help children to *feel* the
      silence while they waited. *And Jesus said unto him,
      Receive thy sight.* (Verse 42.)

CONCLUSION : Question carefully, to lead the children to
suggest that when Bartimæus' eyes were opened he would
first see Jesus himself, because he was standing right in front
of him. Then let them *think out* what he might say and do,
and also what the other people might say and do. Then read
to them what the Bible tells us in verse 43.

Things to do:

  (a) Draw or cut out some of the things Bartimæus would
      look at when Jesus had made him see; show and
      discuss what they have done.

  (b) Draw a picture of the story.

  (c) Act the story, letting children take it in turn to be
      Bartimæus. Teacher to read words of Jesus from
      Bible.

The above is the ground plan of a lesson, and whatever
the subject, or the method employed, and for whatever age,
the same kind of lesson plan can be used. Each part could be

entirely different, but the layout would be the same, so that it could be seen at a glance what kind of lesson it was intended to be. In fact, it should be possible for a teacher, who was suddenly unable to give a lesson, to send the lesson notes to a substitute teacher without having to add any further explanations. The Aim of this lesson shows at once what the teacher is to do; the headings show clearly the points to be dealt with; and the brief notes show how the lesson is to be given.

If lesson notes are being prepared in columns, the Presentation Stage will appear like this:

SUMMARY	METHOD
1. THE BLIND MAN'S DAILY LIFE	
(a) *His Home.*	Tell his name and let children repeat it. Show model house. Describe city wall and gate. (Draw on blackboard.) Tell how he left home each morning and went out through gate, perhaps feeling his way with a stick.
(b) *His Begging.*	Describe. Suggest he may have sat under a palm tree. (Draw him sitting there.) Picture him listening to sounds around him, and describe them (with actions where possible): people's footsteps, trotting donkeys, padding camels; voices of people gossiping and telling him news; the sound of money dropping into his bowl.
(c) *His Return Home.*	At end of day he counts his few pennies and taps his way home. (Rub figure from blackboard.)

The notes would continue in this way throughout the Presentation Stage.

So far we have been considering the building up of lesson notes, but this is only a part of our preparation of a lesson. The other points to be considered can be put under two headings, (1) during the week before the lesson, and (2) immediately before the lesson.

1. It is important to know, as early in the week as possible, what the next lesson is to be, so that we can have it in our minds and be on the look-out for suitable material to put into it. Little incidents of ordinary life often aptly illustrate some point in a lesson, and being actual experiences of the teacher they will make much more impression on the children than an illustration given in a lesson book. The teacher should always be ready to use local or personal items of interest, provided they are suitable, instead of those suggested in a book, which are necessarily impersonal since the writer does not know the children with whom the lesson will be used.

Then there may be brief extracts from the daily papers that just fit, or pictures that could be cut out and mounted on cardboard, and perhaps coloured. It may often be a good plan to get the background part of our blackboard sketch drawn during the week, so that we can practise giving the lesson with it, and there may be other pieces of apparatus to be prepared. This should all be done in good time.

Where there is a Preparation Class it should always be attended, and each teacher should take an active part in the discussions. Here we can share the information that we have been collecting during the week, so that other teachers can have the opportunity of using it too, and we can also learn from their discoveries.

Another important preparation is to get to know the children we are teaching, and the best way to do this is by visiting them in their homes and making friends with the rest of the family. Teachers who do this know what a tremendous difference it makes in the attitude of the children to the teacher, when they have come to look upon him as a friend of the family. And it also gives the teacher something to talk about with the children, should they happen to meet unexpectedly, if he knows their hobbies and the names of their brothers and sisters. Very often a visit to the home will make all the difference to the teacher's understanding of a difficult child, and will enable him to deal sympathetically with him.

Most important of all, it is necessary to realize how entirely unable we are to fulfil our task as teachers in our own strength. So a large portion of our preparation time will be spent in "talking it over with God", telling him of our plans and hopes, our difficulties and disappointments; remembering each one of our children in our prayers, and asking help and guidance for ourselves. Our Lord Jesus Christ was a Teacher, and we like to think of him as the Perfect Teacher whose example we long to follow. We can only follow an example if we are familiar with it, and so perhaps the best preparation of all is to read the Gospel accounts of the Life of our Lord and spend a little time picturing the scenes and letting our thoughts dwell upon them until we have caught something of his enthusiasm and learnt some of the secrets of his success.

2. On the day itself, when the lesson is to be given, we must be very practical. It is better not to try to make any last minute alterations in the lesson, unless we discover an error, or some exceptionally good idea should occur to us. Apart from this we should be content to feel that we have done our best, and to trust that God will accept our offering and make good its shortcomings. Our main concern on the day itself should be with the external arrangements. Religious instruction is given in many different organizations and buildings, and some teachers have a room to themselves for the lesson period, while others have to share a crowded room with many other classes. Something can be done to improve even the worst conditions, and the first need is for the teacher to arrive in time to do whatever is practicable, and to have all arrangements completed, before the time for the children to be admitted. For this he could have volunteer helpers from among the more punctual children, so long

as they know for what particular jobs they are responsible.

The teacher must see that everything needed for the lesson, either by himself or by the children, is ready to hand before the session starts, so that there will be no disturbance or delay once the lesson has begun. And the children should be arranged so that each one can both see and hear the teacher. The best formation is a half circle or, if forms are used, three sides of a square, or two sides of a triangle, with the teacher far enough back for the child at either end to be well within his view, thus :

Avoid having the teacher's chair too near to the children, like this :

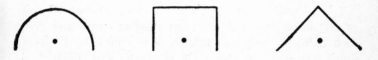

as it allows the children at the end to be out of sight and hearing, and to feel cut off. This will leave them with nothing to do but play. But if these end seats are well in view they can be used for the more troublesome children.

A second chair on the teacher's left hand can be very useful as he can keep his books on it, and also rest a small hand blackboard there, where the children can easily see it.

CHAPTER 7

CHARACTERISTICS OF CHILDREN AGED TWO TO FIVE YEARS

WE have been considering the interests of children of varying ages, and trying to see how a knowledge of these can
help us to know what it is reasonable to attempt to teach
them at each stage of their development. We now have to
go on from a consideration of the things *outside* a child
which attract him, to a study of the life *within* the child, and
so to an understanding of the way in which the child
responds to outside events.

As we have already realized, a child is not just an empty
jar into which we can pour knowledge, but a personality
with definite characteristics, and he will of necessity make a
characteristic response to everything that comes into his
experience. A knowledge of these characteristics will enable
us to plan our teaching so that we can get from the child the
response we want him to make.

It is a well-known fact that no two children are ever
exactly alike, except in very rare cases of twins, and even
then there are personal differences of character, however
much they may resemble each other externally. Each child
is a living soul, able to have a personal relationship with
God and with his fellow members of the human race. It is,
therefore, not possible to give an exact description of the
characteristics of any particular group of children, and we
must content ourselves with considering a few of the more
general ones that are normally to be found in each of the
age-groups.

How are these to be discovered? It is not easy for an
adult to understand the mind of a child, and see, feel, and

interpret external things in the same way as the child does himself. There are three ways open to us, and we should to some extent use all three, while not relying too completely on any one of them, since all are exposed to the same danger of being understood in terms of the adult mind rather than those of the child.

The first way is by observation—we can observe children in their various activities and see how they respond : (a) to different things at the same age, and (b) to the same things at different ages. From these two experiments, if carried out over a fairly long period of time, we can often get a good deal of useful information. It is very important that the children should not know that they are being observed, otherwise their responses will not be natural. Even a very young child will show off if he realizes that he has an audience of interested adults. But if we make friends with children, and do with them the things they like to do, we can watch without their realizing it, and make our own mental notes.

Whenever possible, visits should be made to organizations where children can be seen at work and at play, such as Children's Clubs, Brownie and Cub Meetings, Sunday and Day Nursery Schools, etc. Children can also be watched at play in school playgrounds, public parks, and private gardens. It is useful to record the results of such investigations in a note-book, and to compare them with information gained in other ways.

The second way of learning about children's characteristics is by trying to remember what we ourselves were like as children. This is a less satisfactory way than the first, because we are almost certain to read back much of our later experiences into the earlier memories, and thus see ourselves less as we really were than as we think we must have been. Yet some memories from childhood are so vivid that we can be practically certain that we really did think and act in a particular way, and with practice this method can become very helpful to us in the understanding of other children.

The third way is by studying, and learning what we can from the results of the many tests and experiments that have been made by those who make a special study of Child Psychology.

It is a good plan when reading someone else's discoveries to test them from one's own knowledge of actual children, saying, "Yes, I can see little Betty doing that", or "I am sure that would not work with John!"

Here we shall deal mainly with the first method, that of observation, and the reader is advised to supplement from personal work along the lines of the other two.

The first group to be observed is that from two to five years of age. These children are emerging from babyhood and beginning to develop considerable independence, and to do many things without being prompted. It is, therefore, possible to discover certain things about them from their behaviour.

Let us imagine that we are staying with a family where there are two children in this age group—David 4 and Jean $2\frac{1}{2}$. They are together most of the time, and have a number of toys: coloured blocks for building, woolly animals, wooden trucks that they pull or push about and fill with toys. As we watch them at play we see that they do not play *together*, even when they are both doing the same thing. They will not take very much notice of each other unless one of them wants something that the other has. For the most part they will each be quite happily occupied with one thing after another, each taking the other for granted, but making no demands of any kind.

If we ask either child whose toy it is that he or she is playing with, we shall get a similar answer: David will probably say, "Mine", and Jean will more probably say, "Jean's". And we shall find that this claim to personal possession will extend to everything that forms a part of their daily life. It will be, "My house", "Jean's garden", "My Daddy", "Jean's Mummy", and we shall learn that David and Jean own individually all the various things that make up the home.

A friend with a car came to spend a few days at a house where there was a little girl about the age of Jean. She stoutly declared that it was "Mary's car", and quite genuinely believed that it existed entirely on her account.

From all this we can learn a very important fact about children of this age : they are in the very centre of their own little world : everything in it is there because they need it, and other people are just a part of that same world which revolves about them. In this world they are very interested, so much so that they claim it as entirely their own, and they quite confidently expect everything in their world to be equally interested in them. In other words, they are ego-centric, which means, "self in the centre", from the Latin word *ego*, meaning I, or self. This characteristic of being the centre of one's own world is called *egoism*, and the child in this two to five age-group is an egoist.

This does not sound a very pleasant characteristic, and in an older person it is most unpleasant and undesirable. But in the little child it is natural and reasonable. The child is so small in a very large world, and other people are so much bigger than he is ! If he were able to realize that they had an existence apart from him, and that a vast world was going on beyond his little circle, without any concern for him at all, it would be very terrifying indeed. He is so helpless and de-pendent that it is of the utmost importance that he should feel safe and at home in his world, and it is a merciful provi-sion of nature that he is only able to be aware of what is happening within his own sight and hearing. Great care should be taken to do nothing to destroy this natural protec-tion of the small child, but rather to take it into account and use it as a valuable guide in making plans for teaching him.

There is another side to this. The fact that his world revolves around him makes the child naturally expect that it will be ordered to meet his needs and wishes, and to meet them at once. There must be a keen sense of shock, and a first dawning sense of insecurity, when his world fails to do this. His sudden outbursts of rage, when thwarted, are probably much more due to surprise and fear than to self-will, because we find that the little child is usually very ready to fall in with a suggestion of "Shall we do . . ." or "Let's go and . . ." It is the suddenness of adult interference, or the unexpectedness of refusal, that frightens him and throws him into a rage. One woman remembered all her life a childhood's shock of terror on being suddenly picked up, when walking along, and dumped into a perambulator.

In some cases it is not persons, but things, that thwart a child, and his helpless rage with a toy that will not do what he wants causes him to smash it. But this is not so much from a wish to destroy it as from a need to assert himself and recover his sense of security. It is a natural thing to strike out at the thing that threatens our security, and to the little child anything that defies him does this.

It is therefore very important not to interfere in any way with what a small child is doing without giving him warning and, whenever possible, gaining his willing co-operation. This requires much patience, and we shall not always be able to avoid tears, because even at this early age the child must begin to learn that things cannot always be as he wishes. But we can, and should, avoid making him afraid and therefore angry.

Another thing to be remembered is that he has no sense of time. Everything with him is *now*, and so it is of little use to say to him, "You shall have it back again presently". If it is necessary for him to give something up for a time, he must be persuaded to do so, and it can then be offered to him again later on. If by then he no longer wants it, it will not matter.

To return to David and Jean : we noticed that they spent some of their time pushing or pulling their trucks about; sometimes, but not always, putting other toys into them. If we watch this for some time we shall see that Jean seems to be continually changing her activities without achieving anything at all. First she will put some blocks into her truck and begin to pull them along; then she will take them out and pull the truck for a few moments without them; then she will laboriously load it up again, only to put the blocks out a moment later. Again, she will seem to pull the truck aimlessly about the room, without any apparent intention of taking it anywhere. David's behaviour will be much the same except that he may play a game of pretence, saying that he is the baker and the blocks are loaves, and inviting us to buy some. But even so there is little obvious purpose in the game, which may stop abruptly with the loaves still unsold.

Thus we can see that at this age there is considerable activity, but with little apparent purpose. The child moves about from the sheer love of movement without needing any further inducement. And this, again, is quite natural and reasonable, for he is growing rapidly and the same energy that promotes this growth also stimulates activity. In fact, it would be impossible for him to remain for long inactive, and very harmful if he were made to do so by force. This characteristic of *activity with little purpose* must also be catered for when a lesson is being prepared.

We have already noticed that while playing with one set of toys, the child at this age will be constantly changing his activity. He will also be continually changing his occupations, never doing any one thing for very long. Jean will suddenly leave her truck in the middle of a journey round the room and begin to play with her teddy bear. After taking great pains to tuck him up comfortably in bed she will immediately take him up again, and a few minutes later leave him uncomfortably on the floor while she plays with a coloured ball.

David will change his occupations almost as often; he will suddenly stop building operations and dash out into the garden, where he will charge up and down, "being an engine". After a short time he will begin digging in his own piece of garden, or in the sand pit if there is one. But he will not keep to anything very long. Neither he nor Jean are able to keep their minds upon one thing for any length of time, and a sudden new idea will at once start them off on a new activity. This, too, should be noted, and provision made for their *love of change and variety* when teaching these little ones.

We have noticed a good deal about what these small children do. If we are with them for long we may be struck by the fact that Jean does not *say* very much, and what she does say is often repeated many times. This is what we shall expect when we remember that all children have to learn a language before they can speak it. At the age of two years the child has only learnt a very small number of words, and is not always very sure of their use. We shall probably hear Jean practising some of the newer words that she has learnt, and also saying to her dolls some of the things her mother has been saying to her. But she will find it difficult to put into words the things she wants to tell us, and it will be much easier for her to show us what she means than to tell it. Even David will more readily make use of his hands than of his tongue when trying to explain what he has been doing, or is trying to do. As the nursery child has such a *very small vocabulary*, and can only understand very simple words, we should not only make a point of saying "Show me" as often as possible instead of "Tell me", but we ourselves must be careful to show, by our actions, what we mean by the words we use.

There is another point about words which is not always realized. Many words do not mean the same thing to a small child as they do to us, because his experience of a thing referred to is different from ours. An easy illustration of this is the word "table". To us it means something with a flat surface upon which we can put things, and the table top is the part of it which is most familiar to us. But to a tiny child a table is something under which you walk or crawl, and where you often sit to play. The child to whom the word "table" means this may not, when sitting in his high chair, realize that the flat surface in front of him is also the table, and there may very well be confusion in his mind if told to put something "on the table".

There is one more important point that we shall notice as we watch these children. If we present Jean with a new, unfamiliar toy she will very probably, if it is small enough, try to put it into her mouth. She will handle and turn it over and over, and perhaps it will be some minutes before she really looks at it. David might also want to lick it, to discover how it tastes, and besides handling and looking at it he will probably give it a good shake, and be delighted if it makes a noise. At this age there seems to be little interest in how things smell, but the other four senses are very alert. When we come to think of it, we shall realize that everything we know we have learnt by the use of one or more of our senses, and that without any of them we should not be able to know anything at all. Helen Keller became deaf and blind when about eighteen months old, but she could still feel, taste, and smell, and it was found to be possible to teach her through her sense of touch, so that people could speak to her on her own hands, and she could also tell what they were saying by putting her fingers on their lips or throat and feeling the vibrations when they talked. If all the senses were to go, nothing could be learnt.

4

While the adult is able to interpret from past experience the thing that he sees and hears, the little child has very little experience to help him, and so has to make an exhaustive examination of everything new that comes within his reach. His senses are always on the look-out for new material to explore, and if this is not supplied his development will suffer. Children who have not been allowed, or able, to have suitable things to play with, are often dull and backward when they reach school age. Their hungry senses have been starved, and their minds and bodies have suffered in consequence.

This *sense hunger* is not only something which needs to be satisfied, it is the most important factor in our teaching of the children, and the only means by which they can receive the truths we want them to learn.

CHAPTER 8

IT IS important to understand the relation between *teaching* and *learning* in order to realize the value of the various methods that can be employed. From the very beginning of our lives, and normally until the end, we are learning by a natural process; and even if no attempt were made to teach us anything, we should acquire a considerable amount of knowledge in the course of a lifetime. But it would be very wasteful if each one of us had to learn everything from experience only, and could not benefit from the experiences and discoveries of the human race all down the ages. It would be ridiculous if each individual had to discover for himself the use of steam or electricity, and it would be equally ridiculous if we all had to discover for ourselves a form of speech, or invent an alphabet or a numerical system. Yet this might have to be done if it were not possible for each generation to hand on to the next the fruits of its experience, and the results of its experiments and discoveries. And this is the true function of teaching. Yet in carrying out this function we must not forget that the natural way of learning is through experience, and if we are wise we shall take this into account and so plan our methods that the children can, whenever possible, discover for themselves that which we want them to learn.

This is especially important with the little ones who have so little past experience of their own upon which to draw, and whose whole existence is, therefore, a voyage of discovery. It is the natural method, and the one they can best understand.

Sometimes a grown-up, wanting to please a small child, will hide something and then tell the child to go and look for it. It is disappointing to find that the child does not respond, but just looks blank. If the grown-up person were to take the child's hand and say, "Come and see what we can find", and put the child in the way of finding it, then the child would enter into the fun and be thrilled with the discovery.

That is how we must teach these little ones : not just tell them and expect them to be interested, but take them with us within reach of the thing to be discovered, and then let them find it for themselves. In other words, we must put the necessary material within their reach, and then wait patiently for them to make use of it.

This means that, for the Nursery Child, there will be very little actual instruction given, but a very great deal of apparatus will be needed. So perhaps the first method to be considered should be the use of apparatus.

For a Sunday Nursery School the question of apparatus will depend very largely on the size of the school. In many cases it may only be a Nursery Class, consisting of the youngest children in the Kindergarten. These would perhaps share in the greater part of the Kindergarten programme, and then be taken to their own classroom for the lesson. When this is so, we shall only need to consider what apparatus can be used for a lesson. Where there is a separate Nursery School, the apparatus and equipment are the responsibility of the Superintendent, who should have some definite qualifications and training in nursery-school methods. The teacher of a nursery *class* will, therefore, have more responsibility, but less scope, than one of many teachers in a nursery *school*. As this also applies to those who teach any small group of children, it will be more helpful if the discussion of apparatus be mainly confined to that which can be used in giving a lesson.

When possible it is well to have little chairs on which the

children can sit, with their feet firmly planted on the floor. Their legs must not be allowed to dangle. We shall realize at once how this puts a child at a disadvantage if we experiment with ourselves, and try to do something with our hands while perched on a high seat with no support for our feet. As these children should be continually changing their activity, it would cause great confusion if they all had to clamber up and down big chairs every time they wanted to move. If it is not possible to have small chairs it is better to have none at all, but to provide either a thick rug and let them sit on the floor, or small hassocks. These can be made from hessian or other strong material and stuffed with tow, or newspapers with a layer of tow between the papers and the cover. Where there are chairs there should also be low tables taking four to six children.

The teacher must always sit at the same level as the children. This will give the children confidence, and enable them to talk with the teacher without having to be looking up all the time. An adult should never talk to a small child without sitting or kneeling down to his level. A full-grown person bending over a child may have a very forbidding appearance.

In a Day Nursery School all the toys are educational, that is to say, they are so designed that from playing with them the children will be able to make certain discoveries and learn many things without any awareness that they are being taught. They learn that a square peg must fit into a square hole, and a round one into a round hole, by playing with both sorts and a board with both round and square holes in which to put them. As we are not wanting to teach quite the same kind of thing, we shall not use quite the same kind of apparatus, but we can employ the same principle of letting the child play with something that will help him to learn what we want to teach.

APPARATUS

1. *The Sand Tray.*—This is a long-established favourite which has not outlived its usefulness. With very little children it is better to have one big tray for the teacher to use while the children sit round it and watch, than for each child to have a small one. Their imaginations are not yet sufficiently developed for them to be able to invent scenes, but they can follow a simple story worked out in the tray, and then either do the end of the story themselves or do it all while the teacher goes over the story again. A big tray also makes it easier to have the models large enough for the children to handle them and discover what they are like.

An example of this way of using a sand tray would be the telling of the story of the Lost Sheep. If the children have small chairs and tables the tray should be of a size to fit comfortably on the table, and deep enough to allow the sand to be heaped up to make small hills. The sand should be slightly damped, so that it will keep in place. In one corner there would be a sheep fold, and inside it some toy sheep. (It is possible to make small sheep out of pipe cleaners, and they can sometimes be bought ready made at art and craft shops.) There should also be a shepherd, who could be made from a wooden clothes peg, and dressed like an eastern shepherd. Stones for boulders, and green stuff for food, should be added.

The story would be very simple and quite short, the Aim being to show how the shepherd takes care of his sheep. First the children could be shown the sheep and allowed to handle them, and names could be chosen for them. Then they could be put to bed in the fold, and the children be introduced to the shepherd, who would then be put to sleep across the door of the fold, "To keep the little sheep safe".

There need be no pause for the passing of night—small children know nothing of the passing of time while they sleep. So the story-game can go on at once to waking up, and the shepherd will get up and call each sheep by name, and when they are all outside he will lead them off to find their breakfast. So shepherd and sheep will be moved about the tray up and over the hill, and then one of the sheep will stray away from the rest and get lost. Now it is time to go home to bed, and the shepherd leads the way back to the fold, and counts the sheep as they go in. Now comes the exciting part, for there is one short, and the children will have to go over the names to find out which one is missing. Then will follow the search, with the children calling the name of the lost sheep, and the shepherd hunting everywhere but in the right place. This must not go on too long; the teacher must judge from the behaviour of the children when to reach the climax of discovery, after which there should be the hurried return and an extra careful putting to bed of the tired sheep. The suggestion all through must be that the sheep is really quite safe because the shepherd is looking for it.

The story can be repeated, using exactly the same words, while the children now move the shepherd and sheep about, or the children can be allowed to play their own game with the sheep. Though they will not play a corporate game, they will quite happily play their own separate games in the same tray, if it is large enough.

2. *Models.*—However large the tray, the figures used will have to be rather small. But it is possible to use models without a tray, and then they can be considerably larger. For little children these should be mainly figures—people, especially children, animals and birds, flowers and trees. One very good method is to mount suitable coloured pictures, containing a number of these, on to thick cardboard or plywood and to cut them out. Another large piece of wood or cardboard can then be painted to make a permanent background—a gravelly path in front, green grass behind, and hills in the background. The children can then make a great

variety of scenes with the figures, arranging the flowers and trees to make a garden, and moving the people and animals about to make a story. All the cut-outs lie flat on the background as in an ordinary picture, but they have the advantage of being movable, while the same background will serve a number of purposes.

Models of this kind could be used in telling about the finding of the baby Moses; and if each child had a set he could play the story over and over again, making his own arrangement of the figures.

One of the uses of figures in a Day Nursery School is to help the children to learn to recognize things that are similar. There will be models of two sheep, and a tiny lamb; a bull, a cow, and a calf; a duck, a drake, and a duckling, etc. These are all put together and the children are encouraged to sort them out into families.

Something similar to this could be done with figures for the Christmas story : there would be Joseph, Mother Mary, and the Baby Jesus; three shepherds; perhaps three sheep and three goats; some cows and donkeys. After hearing the story the children would be asked to find the different characters and to build up the Crib Scene with them. For this it would be better to have figures that stand up, and they could be made to do so either by gumming a small wooden block behind the foot of each figure, or by making a slot in the black into which the figure could be fitted.

3. *Pictures.*—These should be large, clear, and of good strong colours, with very little detail. They can be bought, but it is often better for Nursery School teachers to make the pictures, because they can then have in them only the things that are wanted. One way is to cut out from a picture, and paste on to a sheet of suitably coloured paper, the particular objects about which we want the children to learn. Or the objects can be cut in silhouette from paper of one colour and pasted on to that of another. Teachers who have any

drawing ability can easily learn to make very attractive blocked-in pictures with coloured chalks. Outline pictures drawn on a blackboard are not suitable for these young children as they need to see things in a solid block. A mother drew the outline of a teapot on a piece of paper and was surprised that her little boy of $2\frac{1}{2}$ could not recognize it. When she shaded it in the child said at once, "teapot".

The pictures can be used in a variety of ways : in a large picture the various objects can be covered up, and uncovered by the children one by one as they come into the story; there can be a series of pictures one over the other, showing different stages of the story, which can be turned over as the story progresses; pictures can be arranged to make a frieze and the children allowed to walk along looking for the objects that make up the story. Whatever method is used, the children should do all the pointing out and naming, the teacher sitting beside the picture to give encouragement.

As pictures are fragile the children should not handle them; nor should small pictures be used, as they strain the eyesight of little children.

4. *Real Things.*—The apparatus so far described is a part of the permanent equipment of a Nursery School. For many types of lesson, especially nature lessons, it is possible to show the children the real things. These would be provided for the one occasion only. Sometimes they would have to be combined with life-size models of objects which could not be obtained. For example, in a lesson on bird life, to show how the father and mother bird care for their young, it might be possible to show the children a real bird's nest, and let them see how beautifully it is lined to make a soft, warm bed for the tiny eggs. But it would not be at all a good thing to show them real eggs, because that would entail the destruction of bird life. We could make some model eggs out of clay or plasticine, or we might even be able to get sweets made like eggs. Then for flower and plant lessons we can

have the real flowers and let the children see how carefully the little buds are wrapped up; or the real plants, and show them all the different parts. In a lesson on food we can have actual food, and let the children taste it; sometimes we might bring real creatures, such as dormice, snails, birds, or tiny chicks. All these have been used successfully with small children, to teach how the Heavenly Father takes care of all little things.

5. *Materials for the Children's Own Use.*—In addition to the permanent and occasional apparatus there must be material for the children to use, and *use up*. Though they are not yet at a creative stage they have a great love of *doing*, and we must provide opportunity for this. Plasticine and clay are great favourites : the children may do little more than roll it in their hands, but they will generally tell you what they have made. Others like to draw, and this is best done with crayons on coloured paper, or with coloured chalks on a small blackboard. The drawings will be little more than scribble, but to the children they are pictures. Older children can be very happy with a sheet of coloured paper which they can cut or tear into shapes representing animals and people, and then arrange into a picture. By cutting folded paper they can make a frieze.

Unless it is known that the parents will be able to enter into the spirit of the teaching it is better not to let the children take their drawings, etc., home. If they were ridiculed the drawing would no longer be spontaneous and its value would be destroyed.

CHAPTER 9

METHODS OF TEACHING THE NURSERY CHILD—II

STORY-TELLING. In describing the various forms of apparatus that can be used, reference has continually been made to *the story*. In a Day Nursery School there may be one period in the day when stories are told, but for the greater part of the day the children are engaged in free play. In a Sunday Nursery School children come for an hour at most, and if there is to be a story it will necessarily have a much more important place than in the day school, and it will also have to be closely related to the other brief activities of the children. Generally the story is the central feature, but it can be told in a number of different ways along with the use of the various kinds of apparatus already described.

Story-telling is one of the most ancient methods of teaching, much of the earliest knowledge of the human race having been preserved and handed on by means of stories, told by professional story-tellers for many centuries, before they were written down. Yet the story holds an important place in the most up-to-date methods of teaching.

The telling of a story is an art which often has to be acquired, and always has to be practised. Before telling a story to a class it is a good plan to try it out, either with a grown-up friend or a child, or else in a room alone. It can help sometimes to do it in front of a mirror. There are several important rules that must be kept in mind whenever we are preparing to tell a story. These are :

1. The story must be suitable : (*a*) to the age and development of the child, and (*b*) to the Aim of the particular lesson being taught. If we try to tell a story to children for whom

it can have no interest whatever, they will not attempt to listen to it; in a very few minutes they will have found something much more interesting to do, and we shall probably have lost their attention completely. Worse still, we shall have failed to teach them the things we wished them to learn and the whole lesson period will have been wasted.

Again, however interested the children may be in a story we are telling, unless it has a definite bearing on the Aim of the lesson it will teach them nothing, and we shall have failed entirely to accomplish our purpose. So when choosing stories we must have both these important points in mind. Our knowledge of the interests and characteristics of the children will help us with the first, and careful thought will help us with the second.

2. Having chosen a story, the next point is to know it well, so that we can be quite sure we shall tell it correctly, and not leave any important parts out. It is *not* a good plan to learn it by heart, first of all because there will be a tendency to recite it and that will mean loss of naturalness; and secondly because there is a danger of missing out a whole section and not discovering it until too late to put it in. The best way to remember it is to arrange it into scenes, either on paper or in our own minds, and to memorize these but not the actual words in which we are going to describe them. If we arrange the opening and closing words for each scene, then we can make a link in our minds between the last words of one and the first words of the next, and so avoid the risk of leaving a whole scene out. This will also help us to *see* the whole thing happening, so that each scene will naturally follow the one before it.

3. If we want to hold the attention of the children our telling of the story must be dramatic. It is not very easy for anyone to listen to someone else talking, we most of us would prefer to do the talking ourselves, and it is especially hard for children because of their restless physical energy. We have

to try to change this into mental energy, and can only hope to do so if we are really helping them to picture the scenes for themselves, and to feel that they are taking a part in the story. It can help in this way if we make good use of our voice, speaking in a pleasant, cheerful way, and changing our tone from time to time to fit the words we are using. For example, in telling the story of Goldilocks and the Three Bears, our voice should be mysterious when she begins to explore the bears' house, excited when she finds the porridge, soft when she lies down to sleep. Then it will change for the different voices of each of the three bears, and become tense with excitement when Goldilocks leaps from the window and makes her escape.

Another important point is the right use of gesture. This must not be overdone, because children are very quick to respond to the ridiculous, and there is a risk of provoking sudden mirth in quite unsuitable places. But a certain amount of gesture is very helpful, such as pointing out a direction, adopting a listening attitude when telling of approaching footsteps, etc. With little children all the actions of a story can be shown, such as going to sleep, beating up eggs, coming down stairs, sneezing, etc.

One other way of making the story-telling dramatic is by changing the expression of our faces, looking sad or gay, excited or disappointed, according to the development of the story.

4. One of the secrets of success in story-telling is the use of simple language, and this is especially so when the stories are being told to children, whose thoughts are simple and direct. It might be a wise thing to make a rule never to use a word of two syllables if there is an equally good one of one syllable only. Elaborate language tends to confuse and to attract the attention to itself and away from the story, just as a beautiful room can be spoilt if overcrowded with heavy furniture. But the words must be good and well chosen, so that the

telling of the story can be graphic and so make a vivid impression.

5. When telling a story with conversations, give the words of the various characters in direct speech; that is to say, quote the actual words as they were spoken. In the story of Blind Bartimæus say, *Jesus stood still, and said, Call ye him* (Mark 10. 49), and not *And Jesus stood, and commanded him to be brought unto him* (Luke 18. 40). Direct speech gives opportunity for change of voice and makes it easier to listen to the story, as the characters really *live*.

All these rules apply, whatever the kind of story or the age of the listeners. There is another that is important when telling a story to very young children, and that is the use of repetition. These children are learning the words, as well as their meaning, and so take a particular delight in the actual words used, so much so that they remember them and can generally tell at once if we use a different word when re-telling a story. Repetition is a valuable aid to memory, but as children get older and have more experience of life, they are better able to make a picture in their minds of what they are being told, and when eager to know the end of the story they would be bored by too much repetition.

This is the House that Jack built, is an example of the kind of repetition in which the words delight far more than their actual meaning, but there is no reason why both words and meaning should not equally please.

A visitor was once invited to read the children's bedtime Bible story, and was given a book of Bible stories for children. The children's choice was the story of the golden image set up by King Nebuchadnezzar, and the friend began to read. After reading a few lines, she said to the mother, "For goodness sake, give me a Bible", and insisted on reading the unspoilt story as it is written in the third chapter of the Book of Daniel (R.V.). It is an almost perfect story for children, with five sets of repetition, and the most lovely language throughout. The wonderful names—Shadrach, Meshach, and Abednego—are repeated no less than thirteen times; "The image that Nebuchadnezzar the King had set up" is repeated five times; there are two identical lists of eight different kinds of officer, and one shorter list at the end; the words "burning fiery furnace" come in eight times; but best of all is the description of the musical instruments, given four times in exactly the same order, with only one omission in the second list. "The sound of the cornet, flute, harp, sackbut, psaltery, dulcimer, and all kinds of music". Apart from these words the language is absolutely simple.

The younger children were delighted with the joyous repetitions, and the older ones with the actual story. The idea of a fiery furnace had no horror for them because they had no experience of burning, and the dramatic ending satisfied their sense of justice. Above all it is a story of utter faithfulness, dauntless courage, and the victory of right over wrong.

The children's Bible story book had not only left out all the repetitions, but had not even given the names of the instruments, but merely called them "musical instruments"; and the story was told in the same way throughout, with no direct speech and no vivid descriptions.

One would not, however, choose this story when only very young children are present, but one could tell other stories in this kind of way. The story itself should only take a few minutes unless it forms part of a "combined operation" in which several methods are used together. The story will then be broken up by other activities. An example of this will be given later on.

ACTIONS. Closely allied to the method of story-telling is that of teaching by actions, and the value of this method is that it gives the much-needed opportunity for the children to be active. As we saw when discussing their characteristics, they are naturally very active little people, but cannot go on doing the same thing for very long. So plenty of provision must be made for activity, and where possible this should be linked up with the main theme of the lesson.

There are many different ways of using actions in the Nursery School. The simplest is by letting the children do any actions that come into the story. For example, if we speak of ringing a bell, the children can do the ringing movements; washing our hands, brushing our hair, tying up our shoes can all be part of a story.

Then there are the more elaborate ways of going over a story again, with the children doing what the story describes. This could be done after a flower lesson in which the life story of a flower has been told. The children could all pretend they are flowers, crouching down for the beginning and gradually getting taller and taller, stretching out their arms for the leaves, and tossing their hair for petals. They will be quite ready to do this several times, while the story is retold. Or they can be birds, and hop about the room, flapping their arms for wings.

Sometimes there could be a real attempt to act the whole story, as, for example, the story of the Lost Sheep. Instead of the children playing with the sheep in the sand-tray, they could all become the sheep, and follow the story-teller round the room. They would have to decide first of all which child was to be the lost sheep, and this one would be left behind when the others returned to the fold (inside the circle of chairs or hassocks). Then the shepherd would count them all and find one missing, and the children would name the one who was lost. As the teacher set out to find him the children would call out his name, and the fact that they all knew where he was would not in any way spoil the interest and enjoyment. This could be repeated more than once with different children acting the part of the lost sheep.

On one occasion a missionary story was told to a nursery

class, and a picture used showing the missionary leaving a native hut and walking down to the beach, which was in the front of the picture, so that he was seen full face.

After the story the children were asked if they would like to pay him a visit, and the chairs were arranged in the shape of a boat in which the teacher and children "crossed the sea" and found the missionary coming down the beach to greet them. Then they had tea with him and came home again.

At other times the same nursery class combined with the Kindergarten, which was in another room. On a Sunday after Christmas there was a delicate question as to which of the two departments should have the Crib, and the problem was solved in this way. The Nursery Class was to have it, and the story would be told to them very simply, beginning with the Stable and then telling very briefly about the shepherds. At this point, they were to begin singing "Away in a Manger", which was to be the signal for the other children.

They, in the meantime, had been told the story from the point of view of the shepherds, and three of the children had been dressed as shepherds and had acted the part, the Superintendent reading the words of the Angel. When the singing was heard, the Superintendent asked the shepherds if they would lead the way and take them all with them to Bethlehem, and the procession set out and reached the other room just at the right moment. The little ones. who had already visited the Stable, welcomed the shepherds with great delight.

On the following Palm Sunday the procedure was reversed. The story was told to the Nursery Class from the point of view of our Lord and his Disciples at Bethany, and to the Kindergarten from the point of view of the children at Jerusalem. A staircase from the nursery room led down into a lower room where the Kindergarten was held, and after the story the little ones were invited to go with the Lord

Jesus and his friends to the big town. The teacher led the way, carrying a picture of the Triumphal Entry, and as they "came down the hill", the children in Jerusalem set out to meet the procession, and as it reached them welcomed it with waving branches and shouts of *Hosanna*! They then joined the procession, singing all together, *Praise him, praise him, all ye little children*.

Such occasions would be rare, but even with the very young children it is a good thing to mark the great Festivals with an event of this kind, even though they may not be able at the time to grasp its significance. It will make some impression, and as the seasons come round year by year the growing child will come in time to associate extra joyfulness with special times.

MUSIC. Many of the children's actions can be greatly helped by music, and in one form or another music can play a very important part in the Nursery School. Although it is primarily the concern of the Superintendent and the pianist, it is well for others to appreciate its value, especially those who are musical, as they may at any time suddenly be called upon to take the place of an absent pianist.

One of the simplest uses of music is as a means of suggesting to the children that it is time for certain things to be done. They can very quickly be taught to recognize a signal, which can be single notes or simple variations on two or three notes, or it can be a chord or series of chords, or again it could be a short tune like the signature tunes used on the radio by some of the artists.

The object of using signals of this kind is (a) to arouse the children's interest in the next occupation, and (b) to secure an orderly change over from one activity to another. Each activity would have its own signal.

Another way of using music is for free expression. The children are left perfectly free, and suitable music is played. One by one the children will leave what they are doing and begin to move about with rhythmical movements suggested by the music. A skilful player can get a whole class responding to changing music—now slow, now gay; and the little ones will really be giving expression to their thoughts and feelings in a way that is very satisfying to small people who find it difficult to put these things into words. It will also encourage the shy child to "let himself go," and so feel more at home in his world.

There can also be special, familiar pieces of music with which the same actions are always associated. For example, there will be "flower music", and "bird music", to which the children pretend to be flowers growing up, or birds flying about, and as soon as they hear the music they will respond to it. Similarly there can be sunshine or rain music, and other tunes for running, hopping, swimming, sleeping, etc.

Nursery children will be able to learn a few hymns, though not more than one or two verses should be taught. But the more satisfactory singing for these little ones is in the form of Singing Games, in which the children form a ring and sing to the actions of a game or story. There are two very useful books for this purpose : *Singing Games from Bible Lands*, Saunders, and *Ring Games*, Llewellyn.

The musical instrument need not be a piano. Where there is only a Nursery Class it may not be possible to have a room with a piano. Quite a number of children learn to play the violin, and although they may not all have grown up into musicians, a good many of them must be able to play well enough for the signals and ring games, even if they could not manage the eurythmics.

Anyone who is at all musical can learn to play on an ordinary whistle pipe, and the tune can be very sweet. So the Nursery School need not be without this valuable accompaniment to many of its activities.

Valuable suggestions for work in the Sunday Nursery can be found in *The Under Fives—Suggestions for the Sunday*

Nursery, by Vera Peake, published by The Church Information Board.

CHAPTER 10

As THESE children are so active, and need such continual change of occupation, no one thing can be done for very long. It is, therefore, not possible to have a set programme, with definite times for doing this and that. All the activities will overlap and intertwine, and some of the time will be given up to free play for which no plan can be made. Nor is it easy, on paper, to give a very satisfactory picture of the kind of thing that can be done.

In the Nursery Class the ordinary teacher has more opportunity for planning a programme than in a Nursery School, where this is in the hands of the Superintendent, who would have a plan to submit to the Teacher's Preparation Class, where it would be discussed.

Here is an illustration of what could be done with a small class with only one teacher, though there might be a few helpers who are not yet old enough to teach.

There will be a pianist, fiddler, or piper.

The Lesson is to be about flowers, and the Aim is, "To show how God cares for the growing flowers."

We will imagine a sunny afternoon in Spring, just when the daffodils are coming out in the gardens. (The teacher will have to be prepared with an alternative introduction in case it is not sunny.)

On arrival the children should have their hats and coats removed, to allow them freedom of movement. At the usual signal they will take their places wherever the chairs or hassocks have been arranged, and the teacher will say a few words of welcome and then suggest that, "We tell Heavenly

Father how glad we are to be here". If the floor is covered the children might kneel for the short prayer, either said by the teacher alone or repeated by the children, a sentence at a time. (When children, whatever their age, are asked to repeat a prayer, each sentence used must be complete and have a meaning, otherwise the children will only be repeating nonsense.)

Dear Heavenly Father, thank you for taking care of us all the week. We are so glad to be here to-day. We love you with all our hearts. Amen.

The teacher will then talk about the sunshine, and suggest that they all go and stand in the patch of sunshine on the floor. There they can hold their hands out to the sun and feel its warmth, and the teacher will tell them the sun helps them to grow and to be well and strong. This again can lead to the thought of thanksgiving, and the children can sing either the *Thank him* verse only, or all three verses of the hymn, *Praise him, praise him, all ye little children*, with appropriate actions for each verse.

A signal will take them back to their chairs, and the teacher will talk about the flowers on the table, telling the children that they love the sunshine, too, and that it makes them grow tall and strong. The children can smell the flowers and tell their names. Some of them will be daffodils.

Then will begin the story. "There was a little boy named Jacky, and he had a tiny garden all his very own." Show picture of a little boy in a garden and let one of the children come and point out Jacky.

"One day Jacky's mother gave him something to plant in his garden and told him it would grow into a lovely flower. It didn't look much like a flower, it looked like this." Show bulb, and ask if children know what it is.

"So Jacky planted it in his garden, and watered it every day. Show me how Jacky would water his garden." Let children do action with imaginary watering cans.

"In the morning Jacky said to his mother, 'Let's go and see if the flower has grown'. So they went out into the garden together; but there was no flower, only the brown earth. So Jacky watered his garden again." (Repeat actions.)

"And the next morning Jacky said, 'Let's go and see if the flower has grown'. But there was no flower, only the brown earth. So Jacky watered his garden again." (Repeat actions.)

"Until at last one morning when Jacky said, 'Let's go and see if the flower has grown', and they went into the garden together, they saw . . . Let's go and see what Jacky and his mother saw."

Lead the children to a corner where a sand-tray has been prepared with some brown earth in it and one little spike of green from a bulb showing above the earth. Show it to the children and let them say what it is. Continue the story round the sand-tray.

"Yes, they saw the little green leaves, and Jacky's mother said to him, 'Inside the leaves is a dear little flower bud. Heavenly Father has given it the green leaves to keep it warm'. But there was no flower, only the green leaves and the brown earth. So Jacky watered his garden again.

"When Heavenly Father gave soft rain, then Jacky did not need to water his garden; when Heavenly Father gave warm, golden sunshine, then the little green leaves grew up straight and tall.

"Then one day Jacky could see the bud, on a long stem above the leaves, like this." Show an unopened daffodil bud, let each child see the little warm shawl in which it is wrapped, and then let one of the children put it in the sand-tray. Continue the story: "One sunny morning soon after this Jacky said to his mother, 'Let's go and see if the flower has grown', and they went into the garden together . . . and it had!" (Stoop down and put a fully open daffodil in the tray.) "Jacky was so delighted, he began to sing and dance for joy. At bedtime Jacky said a great big 'Thank you' to Heavenly Father."

If the children know any suitable flower song or hymn they could sing it. The first two verses of *All things bright and beautiful* would fit in quite well, if known, or a new hymn could be taught, such as:

> Heavenly Father makes all the bright flowers:
> Primroses, cowslips, and daffodils tall.
> Warm, golden sunshine and soft rain he gives,
> Lovingly tends them and cares for them all.
> (Tune 52, *Child Songs*.)

(When teaching a hymn the *whole verse* should be sung to the children two or three times, and then they should be encouraged to join in with the teacher, and finally to sing it without her. If the tune is not known, let the children listen to it, and hum it, before trying to sing the words.

With this hymn the names of the flowers can be changed to fit the seasons.)

After singing the hymn the children could go back to the sunny patch and pretend to be flowers growing in the sun, as already described on page 74; the flower music could be played and the children allowed to dance to it round the room.

The signal could then be given for free play, and the children would be quite free to do what they liked, having a choice of walking round to look at pictures on the wall, hung low to be within their reach; looking at a picture book; playing with a sand-tray (not the one with the daffodil), or with cut-outs and a background; drawing; playing with plasticine; or doing nothing at all.

The session would end with a signal for a return to the chairs; another hymn, perhaps *Thank you for the world so sweet*; another prayer, perhaps one that is familiar to the children; and some form of blessing, either said by the teacher or sung by all.

This is one example of how a story can be intermingled with activities, and also of how the Nursery Child's need for frequent change of occupation can be combined with a lesson.

CHAPTER 11

CHARACTERISTICS OF CHILDREN AGED FIVE TO SEVEN YEARS

At the age of five the child leaves the Nursery School for the Kindergarten, but there is no sudden change in the child himself. He is, and for some little time will be, much the same person that he was during the last few weeks in the Nursery, although he is a very different person from the little child of two or three who first joined the Nursery School. This is because children are changing all the time, and the children in any one age-group at any given time are all at different stages of development. The differences will be seen more clearly if the children in the middle of each group are considered, rather than those at either end.

For the purpose of discovering the characteristics of the Kindergarten Child we should, therefore, study mainly the child of six years, though we must not forget that this group also contains the five and seven year olds. Nor must we only study him when he is by himself, for it is not normal for the child of this age to be much alone. As we noticed when studying his interests, he is beginning to make friends, and we shall see him at his best with children of his own age.

If we were to watch a group of children about six years old, boys and girls playing together, we should first of all be impressed by their tireless activity, a much more vigorous activity than that of the Nursery Child. A great amount of energy is being expended in a number of different ways, but after a time we shall recognize some sort of pattern, and see that it is not all movement the purpose of which is not realized by the child himself, but *activity with a purpose* which is his own. The child no longer climbs or runs merely for the joy of climbing or running, but because he "wants to get there"; the bricks are being removed in a truck because they are required for building operations elsewhere; and a drawing is not just "a man", or "me", but someone doing something or going somewhere, or in other words, carrying out a purpose of which the child is conscious.

This new quality in the child's activity is of tremendous importance because it is now something that can be directed and controlled, at first by those in charge of the child, but gradually, through their guidance, by the child himself. Through his new desire to achieve a purpose he can learn his first lessons in patience and perseverance, perhaps to the tune of the old song, "If at first you don't succeed, try, try, try again". Sometimes older people get anxious and suspicious if a child seems too intent on an occupation, and become convinced that he is getting into mischief, like the over-anxious mother who said, "Go and find out what Tom is doing and tell him not to". We should rather welcome this sign of growing control. A child at this age should be interrupted only for a sufficient reason.

With this new sense of purpose in his activity can be seen the dawn of the *urge to create*, which is part of our spiritual inheritance as children of God, the Creator of all things. The child is not merely playing with his bricks, he is building a house, or a railway station. And the house or station is as real to him as the one he lives in, or from which his father travels every day. With the building of the station he has created all that a station stands for, with trains, passengers, luggage, and their destinations.

And the picture he draws is a real work of art, employing the true art of the artist, the attempt to give expression to something that has already taken shape in the mind.

This creative gift is a very valuable factor in the training of the will because the desire *to make* can be strong enough to hold interest and attention until the purpose has been achieved, and so the seeds of perseverance and persistence are sown.

At this age children will make almost anything out of something else, and they should be kept supplied with suitable material for their creative activities.

The creative urge needs the assistance of another characteristic which is now developing, that of *imagination*. This now becomes very fertile and enables the child not only to have a clear picture in his mind of what he wishes to make, and to see in his own handiwork the fulfilment of his purpose, but also to see the possibilities of the various objects that surround him and to gain from them inspiration for games of make-believe. For example, the sudden discovery of a resemblance, in the back of an armchair, to the pulpit in Church will immediately prompt him to convert the whole room into a Church, with his sisters and their dolls as congregation and himself as preacher, by the simple expedient of turning the chair round and climbing into it, and using the back as a book rest. So active is his imagination that the imagined thing is at least as real to him as the actual thing, and often it is more so, with the result that a child of this age may be living in an entirely different world from that of other people who are in the same room as he. This means that a sudden question put to a child may receive an answer that is true in relation to the world in which he is at the moment living while not being true in fact; but because of the reality of that world it is true *to him*. Adults must be very careful not to accuse such a child of lying, but should wait until they are sure that the child is now "himself" and then put the question again. When the true answer is given it can be pointed out that the first answer was not "truly true".

Yet the child does really know the difference between the imagined and the real. A small boy once took a visitor to see a pool in the rock garden. There were several narrow paths leading to it and he led her along each of them in turn, saying every time, "Here is another pool just like the other one. Now I will show you another". When all the paths had been tried he said, "Isn't it wonderful that we have so many pools all just alike?" Yet all the while it was quite obvious that it was only a game, and that he knew it was the same pool each time.

An adult can often enter into the spirit of a game of make-believe, but should be careful not to be too realistic as it is possible to arouse, in an imaginative child, a fear that the imagined may become the real, and that he will not be able to get back. This is what happened to Alice in the book, *Through the Looking-Glass*, by Lewis Carroll; the imagined inside-out world became real and there seemed no way of getting back.

This gift of imagination will enable children to enter into a story and imagine themselves to be characters in it, so that it becomes a real experience to them and makes a lasting impression on their minds. We must be careful, however, not to allow what is imagined to be more attracive than what is real, and thus become an end in itself. Imagination is a valuable instrument only if properly used, so that it can enrich experiences in real life. The Conclusion stage of a lesson provides the opportunity for linking what has been learnt, in the story, to the children's everyday life.

But one cannot imagine out of nothing, and in most of their imaginings children are pretending to be someone else whom they know, or about whom they have heard. In other words they are imitating, and *imitation* is another of the characteristics of this age. We can never be sure who, or what, a child is at any particular moment when living in a world of his own imagining; but at other times, too, a child will either unconsciously or deliberately imitate other people. A boy will want to carry a stick, or an attaché case, "Like Daddy", or a girl to roll pastry, "Like Mummy". Often we are amused to see little tricks and mannerisms faithfully reproduced by the six-year-old. This gift of imitation can be used to develop desirable qualities by suggesting that the child should do this or that, to be like someone he already likes or admires. This last point is important, for unless the person to be copied already has the child's approval the attempt will be a failure and either produce the opposite result, or the child will come to dislike the suggested model.

How is it that a young child knows so much about his world that he is able to imagine all these situations, and play so many parts? He must know far more than he has ever been actually taught, and know it well enough to reproduce it.

The answer to this question can be found in his natural gift of *curiosity* which urges him irresistibly to seek and explore. It is at this age that the child exhausts the adult with his perpetual questions; but it is also owing to this curiosity that he is able to learn at all, for he *can* only learn the things he wants to know, and his curiosity is making him want to know a great many things, as we can see from his characteristic question, "What is it for?"

This, then, is the time to put him in the way of discovering simple facts about religion and life; and it is a fairly safe rule to assume that he is ready to know the true answer to any question he may ask, although we must be careful to give him an answer that he can understand, using as illustrations things with which he is already familiar. Should he ask what the coal is for that he sees in the tender of a steam-engine, we need not describe to him the mechanism of the internal combustion engine, but can demonstrate the power of steam with an ordinary kettle on a coal fire or a gas ring, and tell him the story of James Watt. The answer must always be the truth, and nothing but the truth, but it need not, and often should not be the whole truth.

But the child will sometimes ask us a question to which we do not know the answer and then there is only one thing to be done—we must quite simply say that we do not know and, if possible, suggest that we try to discover the answer together. The child will not despise our ignorance because he will respect our honesty, and he will readily fall in with our suggestion and follow up the enquiry with us because he trusts us, and our frank admission will have further established this trust.

This brings us to another characteristic of this age, *trustfulness*. It is natural for the child to trust and he is ready to believe whatever he is told, without question, unless or until we have given him reason to doubt our honesty. Should we do that we shall not only lose his trust in us, but also undermine his confidence in his whole world.

Two small girls were each promised a ride on a bicycle and the elder was first lifted to the saddle, the cyclist mounted in front of her and they rode off, leaving the younger to wait for their return. The trip was rather longer than had been intended, and on their return the cyclist asked the waiting child, a little guiltily, "Did you think we were not coming back?" The child replied, "I did think you were rather a long time, but I knew you would come back for me *because you said you would*." (N.B. This method of transport is now illegal.)

It is this trustfulness that makes it so very important that a promise made to a child should never be forgotten, and if it should be found impossible to keep it an explanation should always be given. It is equally important that we should never teach a child something that will later on have to be unlearnt. This does not mean that there is no place for such things as fairy stories, for the child knows from his own imaginings the difference between the pretended and the real; but we must never tell him that the fairy stories are true.

There is one more characteristic of the child of this age, which does not always receive the attention that it should.

His new ability to imagine himself as being someone else, together with his own trustfulness, is developing in him a very real power of *sympathy*. The word literally means "feeling with", and because the Kindergarten Child is already coming up against some of the harder experiences of life, he is able to imagine what it feels like when other people have to suffer such things as loneliness, ridicule, misunderstanding, disappointment, etc., and he is often surprisingly understanding in his judgements.

A small boy who was planning the purchase of Easter Eggs for his family came to one of his two aunts and said, "I'm afraid I won't have enough money to buy an egg for you *and* for Auntie Margaret, so I thought I'd better get it for her because I think she'd mind most". An hour later an excited little boy with shining eyes dashed back into the room and held out a paper bag. "Here you are, Auntie", he shouted, "I managed it, I managed it after all!"

Another boy of Kindergarten age noticed that a visitor was being neglected by his elder sister and exclaimed, "Oh, poor Miss C——, she's all alone, I must go to her." After clambering over some obstacles that separated them he sat down very close to her, saying, "Now you won't be lonely any more". A little girl was making Easter Cards for her relatives one year, but insisted that she must also buy a *proper* one for one of them, "Because she's religious".

This characteristic sympathy is important because, through it, we can arouse interest in the work of Missions and Hospitals, etc., and lay the foundations for later teaching on our duty to our neighbour. But we must be very careful not to harrow the feelings of these children by dwelling too much on the aspect of suffering, and must pass on quickly to the means by which the suffering can be relieved. This danger is not very great because at this age children have very little experience of physical suffering, and can only feel deeply about things which they themselves understand. We can tell them about Blind Bartimæus, and the Healing of the Ten Lepers, etc., without distressing them, because the main point in the stories is that the Lord Jesus made them happy.

But there is a very real danger that adults who do not realize the strength of a child's feelings will play upon them in order to get the child to do what they wish. It should never be said to a child, "Do this to please me", for it is making the choice between right and wrong a matter of personal feeling, and should the child happen to forget, and offend, his grief at having vexed someone he loves may be out of all proportion to his wrong-doing, and develop an unhealthy sense of guilt. We want him to learn to choose what is right because it is right, and not merely because it will please us. We must let him see that we like what is good, and are glad *with* him when he has done well; and that we dislike what is bad and can be sorry *with* him when he has done wrong; but we must not give him any reason to think that it can make any difference to our feelings towards him. It can be a really cruel thing to say to a sensitive child, "I am very disappointed in you".

CHAPTER 12

CLASS MANAGEMENT

IN A Kindergarten, methods can be much more directly applied to class teaching than is possible in a Nursery School, as there will be a definite lesson period during which the children are in the hands of their own class teacher. Consideration of methods will, therefore, be mainly confined to those which can be used in classes. The scope of these will necessarily depend to some extent upon the kind of accommodation provided for the Kindergarten, and also upon the number of children in each class. It will be taken for granted that a suitable room is available, and that it is possible to have small chairs for the children, and also that no teacher will have more than six, or at the most eight, children in the class. Teachers who have not these advantages will need to adapt some of the suggested methods to their particular circumstances.

Before considering the various methods a word must be said about Class Management. We are being required to teach a group of children who are full of restless activity, cannot listen very long at a stretch, can only attend to that which interests them, and are only able to learn what they really want to know. Can we hope that they will ever sit still and listen to us? The answer to this is, quite frankly, No! If we expect children at this age to sit still for any length of time and just listen we are doomed to disappointment. But it is possible to get occasional moments of stillness, for example when the climax of a story is reached; and gradually these moments will become more frequent and more sustained, as the children become accustomed to our methods. But this is not our chief aim, and teachers of young children must accept the fact that it is natural for the children to be restless, and that it is almost a necessity for some part of their body to be moving all the time.

An important factor in the art of class management is preparation, and this has already been considered in detail in Chapter 6. All the points made there are important, and could well be revised before reading further.

In addition to careful preparation there are certain points that should be borne in mind at the time of giving a lesson. We must get rid of any idea that we are going to do anything *to* the children, and realize that we are going to do it *with* them, all working together. This will bring us at once into the right relationship with the children, in which they will readily follow our lead because we are travelling with them along the same road. It is a good plan to say, "Shall we", rather than, "Will you", whenever this is possible.

It is generally fairly true to say that we get from people the behaviour which we are expecting. If we expect someone to be easily angered we shall, through over-anxiety, probably do the very thing most likely to anger them; if we are expecting to have difficulties with someone else we shall already be on the defensive before the interview begins, and this will arouse the very antagonism which we have dreaded.

The reverse is also the case, and if we approach a situation with confidence our calmness enables us to establish the right relationships and so avoid unnecessary irritations.

The same principle applies in our relationships with children, we can count on getting from them the behaviour we expect. If a child realizes he is expected to be troublesome he will do his best to oblige; if there is a hint of nervousness on the part of the teacher it will affect the children by making them even more restless than they are naturally inclined to be, and produce favourable conditions for bad behaviour. If, on the other hand, we adopt a manner which shows quite clearly that we are taking it for granted the children are all going to join in and work happily together with us, we shall find that most children will fulfil our expectations. It is much better to do this by our manner than by saying it in words, for although children are very suggestible, that is to say, they will quickly adopt an idea suggested to them by someone else, a suggestion may sometimes have the very opposite effect and put into their minds the idea that it is also possible *not* to do the thing suggested. If a teacher were to say to a particularly active child, "Now let me see how long you can sit still", he would be making it almost impossible for him to sit still at all; and the question, "Are you going to be a good girl this afternoon?" will most probably make a child want to say, "No", and even if she answers, "Yes", and really means it at the time, she will soon yield to the desire to see what will happen if she isn't.

But it is not enough to suggest right behaviour, we must set an example of it ourselves. In all that we do we must be reverent and orderly, and this includes being regular and punctual in our attendance. A teacher must be *regular* in order to make the strong suggestion that the class is so important that he will not allow anything, except illness, to keep him away from it; and also because these young children need routine, and it disturbs them to have, suddenly, to make a new contact. They should have the teacher they are expecting. And the teacher must be *punctual* in order that he may be sure that everything is in readiness; and also to ensure that the children do not arrive to find no one there to receive them. It is a good plan to have something on hand that children who come very early can do, either in the way of helping their teacher, or something they can make for use in the class. If this is not possible, there should be some suitable books for them to look at while waiting for it to be time to begin.

Other points of orderliness are : being ready to start the

lesson immediately the class is settled, so that there is no opportunity for the children to get interested in something else; having all apparatus ready to hand, so that there is no break while the teacher searches anxiously for some missing object; knowing the lesson so well that there is no need to stop to look at notes, which would break the thread and give the children's thoughts a chance to wander away from the lesson subject, with a risk that we might not succeed in bringing them back.

Sometimes we may find that there is not time to finish a lesson, and so we have to leave off before we have been able to make the real point of it clear. At other times we may find ourselves in the still more difficult position of running out of material before it is time to stop. In order to guard against either of these difficulties it is a wise precaution to plan two alternative endings to every lesson we prepare. Lessons given in books are generally designed to help the teachers who get through their material rather quickly, and so need more than teachers who are able to make fuller use of less subject-matter. With most lessons of this kind it is possible to select one portion that could be shortened or even omitted altogether, without spoiling the lesson, and teachers should be prepared to make a quick decision to leave out this part should they find the lesson taking longer than they had expected. On the other hand, those teachers who are liable to finish too soon should come prepared with an additional story or something that the children could do to emphasize the main point of the lesson, which could be fitted in easily and so usefully fill in the extra time.

It only remains to ensure that we have made full provision for the interests and activities of the children we are going to teach, and we should then find little difficulty in holding the children's attention and arousing in them a desire to know what we on our part have a desire to teach. The various methods we can use should help us to fulfil these conditions.

These points on Class Management apply to all class teaching, whatever the age of the children, but their interests and activities will change with their growth and development and, in the case of older children, it will be mental rather than physical activity for which we shall have to cater.

CHAPTER 13

METHODS OF TEACHING THE KINDERGARTEN CHILD—I

STORY-TELLING. As in the Nursery School, the main feature of the lesson will be the story, but in the Kindergarten it can take the form of a connected narrative without being broken up by various activities. This has become possible because of the greater power of these children to give sustained, voluntary attention to anything in which they are interested. So the thing of first importance is to make sure that we gain their interest, and this can most easily be done by bringing into our Introduction something that has already captured their keen interest, and from which we can lead on easily to the lesson story.

There is a good illustration of this in a little book of lessons for young children, *Nature Talks and Stories for the Church's Little Children*, by Millicent Wilkinson. The lesson story is about Good King Wenceslas and it is given as The Story of some Footprints in the Snow. The lesson is intended to be given when there is snow on the ground. As the book is no longer in print, extracts from the lesson are given here.

The AIM of the lesson is : To arouse the children's sympathy for those in need in winter-time, and we shall realize the value of this when we remember the ready sympathy of these little children for the sad and needy.

It is suggested that "a blackboard should be used, the snow drawn on first with the flat side of the chalk, and brown chalk with which to put in the footmarks of the different creatures".

In the INTRODUCTION to this particular lesson a link is made with a previous lesson on a Christmas Tree that grew in the snow, and creatures that have to live in the woods when there is snow on the ground. "Sometimes when we look out at the snow we see little footmarks. We are going to talk about who it is who has been making these little marks."

The children will most probably have noticed the trails of footprints made by all who walk on the snow, whether big or small, and may have puzzled over some of them made by birds or animals. Even in towns there will be the marks of sparrows and robins, cats and dogs. So their interest will already have been aroused and they will be ready to discuss these footmarks. The suggestion is made, "Draw in the small footmarks, and ask whose little feet have made them? A robin or a sparrow perhaps. Add the larger footmarks, and let the children suggest—blackbird, thrush, starling. We can tell this because the marks are bigger. Add the footprints of a rabbit and point out four marks instead of two. Let the children come and add further footprints on the blackboard as the creatures are talked about. Question as to where they are going: To find food and water. Sketch in tree-trunk and make footprints stop there. Sometimes there are little seeds close by the trees, and our Heavenly Father has shown his creatures where to find them. Where do they find water? Sometimes it is very hard to find water, and the birds get thirsty. What can we do to help? Get suggestions from children."

Then follows The Story of Some Footprints in the Snow, beginning in this way: "The story to-day is about a boy who lived in a country where there was always snow on the ground in winter time. He was a servant to the king who lived in the castle on the hill amongst the fir trees. He was called a page boy. The little page often went out in the snow in his big boots and warm cloak. Sometimes he went out with his master the king. He liked that very much. They often saw the footprints of the birds and rabbits in the snow, and sometimes the footmarks of bigger creatures like foxes and the deer when they came near the wood. The king's horse made big footprints too. When it grew dark and cold the page and his master would climb up the hill to the castle. How glad they were to be indoors and to sit by the big fire piled with logs in the hall. One evening, near Christmastime, the page saw his master standing by the window looking out. Presently the page heard his name being called. He ran to the king. 'Stand by me', said the king, 'and tell me who that man is picking up sticks?' The page looked out. The moon was shining and the stars were out, and the snow shone in the moonlight. The page looked at the man. 'I know who he is,' he said; 'he lives a long way off, in a cottage the other side of the wood.' Now the page's master had a loving heart. It made him sad to think of any one being cold or hungry. He was always wanting to help other people, just like the Lord Jesus. 'Run and get some food, and some wine, and some big logs,' he said to the page, 'then you and I will go and take them to that poor man and his family ourselves.'

"The page loved doing things for his master, so he ran off and got a big basket of food ready, and a bundle of logs. Then he and the king put on their big warm cloaks, and they started off down the hill in the snow in the moonlight. The king and the page walked together, the king's big boots making big footprints in the snow, and the page's smaller boots making smaller footprints alongside.

"It was very cold, and soon the page got very tired walking by his master in the deep snow. It seemed such a long way to the poor man's home by the wood. His fingers got so cold, and his feet ached. The cold wind blew round him and under his cloak. The moon went behind a cloud, and the darkness made him a bit afraid. He tried to keep up, but at last he felt he couldn't go any farther. 'Master,' he said, 'it is getting dark, it's so cold. I'm afraid, and I can't go on.' The king turned and looked at the page with kind

5*

eyes, and then at the footprints he was making in the snow.
He felt so sorry for the page boy. 'See my big footprints,
let your feet walk where mine have trod. It will be easier
then.' The page felt braver then, and sure enough walking
in his master's footprints helped him along, and his feet
stopped aching and it didn't seem so cold. At last they came
to the home of the poor man. How surprised the poor man
and his children were to see them, and how glad both king
and page were to open the basket of food, and the bundle
of logs. Their faces shone with love, like the face of the Lord
Jesus. They were happy because they had been able to help
someone who was poor and hungry."

A note to the lesson recommends that, "Opportunity
should be made for the children to do something for those
who suffer from cold or hunger during a hard winter. It
might be possible to save pennies and buy mufflers or blocks
of firewood, or to put food out regularly for the birds, etc."

This is most important because it would be very wrong to
arouse the eager sympathy of little children and then not to
allow them to do anything to help those for whom they were
feeling sorry. It would make them sad and dissatisfied, and
the lesson would have had no value for them at all.

USE OF THE BLACKBOARD. In the story-lesson given above
reference is made to the blackboard, and in the Kindergarten the blackboard plays a very important part. For
the class teacher this will generally mean a hand blackboard, since it is not often that large blackboards and easels
can be provided for every class, and unless the classes also
had separate rooms they would take up far too much space
to be practicable.

There are many ways in which a small hand blackboard
can be used by the teacher of a class.. First of all we must
consider the practical point of how the board should be
handled, for it is important that it should be so held that the
children can see it *while the teacher is drawing, or writing*

on it, otherwise their attention will probably wander away, and instead of being a help it will be a hindrance. The board must be held in the crook of the left arm (or right arm, if the teacher is left-handed), with one side resting firmly against the left shoulder and the other side held about half-way up in the left hand. The left hand should be kept far enough back for the board to be in full view of all the children in the class, and high enough for the board to be straight. It is a good plan to practise this in front of a mirror, to get the *feel* of the board in the right position.

Having mastered this the next step is to try to draw, or write, on the blackboard, and at first it will be found that writing and drawings tend to slope from the top of the shoulder side towards the bottom corner at the other side. To correct this a great deal of practice may be needed because, all the time, there will be a tendency to draw the board round to make it easier to keep the writing straight, and this will bring it out of view of the children. The teacher must persevere with the two things together, keeping the board at the right angle, and also keeping the writing straight across it. Once this has been mastered it will come quite naturally.

We can now go on to consider what can be put on the blackboard when using it with Kindergarten children. For the most part it will be drawings, either pictures or objects. This may sound rather formidable for those who have not considered themselves to be artists, but it will be found that drawing on a blackboard with chalk is very much easier than with a pencil on paper, and there are very few people indeed who are unable to acquire any skill at all with these materials, while most people are surprised to find how quickly they become skilful.

There are two main methods of blackboard drawing— bare outline, and mass work. The first of these is used for quick sketches, such as a background of hills for a story of

Galilee; or for drawing such unfamiliar objects as eastern water-pots, or books. But for little children there is a disadvantage in this method because the picture, or drawing, is like a photographic negative, with the light portions dark, and the dark light. By using the mass method of drawing we can avoid this difficulty, and also represent things not only in black and white, but in their proper colourings.

For this method the side of the chalk is used, and the board, or the required portion of it, covered completely with the chalk, This is then rubbed evenly over the board with the fingers. The picture is made by chalking in more deeply the portions of the picture that should be light, and removing with a duster enough chalk to shadow the darker portions. With the duster stretched over the first finger, and using it as if it were a piece of chalk, thin lines of chalk can be entirely removed, making a black outline round the different objects in the picture to throw them into relief. These pictures take rather longer than an outline sketch, and it might be well to prepare them beforehand, leaving certain details to be added during the lesson. But some people are able to rough in a drawing of this kind very quickly, and when this is the case it is a great joy for the children to watch the development of the picture.

The chief purposes for which blackboard drawings are used in the Kindergarten are :

1. To make a stage on which the details of the story can be worked out. If this is going to require putting in details and rubbing them out again (as in the case of blind Bartimæus), it would be better to have an outline background. But if it is only a case of adding details as the story progresses, a mass picture can very well be used. The children should be encouraged to put in some of the details themselves.

2. To show the children unfamiliar objects, especially such things as eastern houses, and the kind of bed on which

the people of Palestine sleep. Even if an object is familiar, seeing a picture of it drawn can help to arouse the interest of the children in something they take for granted. For example, a town child may really know about farm produce, but he may have become so used to his mother's buying butter and eggs at a shop that he forgets. A sketch showing a cow and her calf, or of a hen with some chicks, will help the child to realize better the way in which our Heavenly Father provides for his children. Such drawings can with great advantage be produced in mass work, and with coloured chalks, and should be prepared beforehand.

3. To teach the words of a hymn or a psalm. For this we shall sometimes use a sketch, adding to it as each thing is mentioned in the hymn; and sometimes we shall draw the different objects as they are mentioned, side by side on the board, so that by referring to them again, in order, we shall help the children to commit the words of the hymn to memory. An example of the first method would be in teaching the hymn, *Over the earth is a mat of green* (Church and School Hymnal, No. 336). First we shall chalk in the green grass, with the side of the chalk, and then add in order, the arching trees, the blue sky, the scudding clouds, and lastly the sun. For teaching the third verse from the hymn, *All things bright and beautiful* (Church and School Hymnal, No. 226), a similar sketch could be made of the purple-headed mountains, the river running by, and to one side of the sketch the setting sun could be drawn; then, when that has been rubbed out, the pink of the early morning could be shown at the other side of the picture. The second method could be used for some other verses of this same hymn, when objects could be drawn : each little flower that opens, each little bird that sings; the ripe fruits in the garden, the tall trees and the rushes, could all be shown in coloured chalks, either in outline or in mass.

In the same way, when teaching the 23rd Psalm, there could either be a country scene as a background for the life of a shepherd and his sheep, or the teacher could draw an eastern shepherd, some sheep, a shepherd's rod and staff; or both methods could be used, one on each side of the blackboard.

The blackboard will be used very little for writing in the Kindergarten, as children of this age are only learning to read quite short words. But the names of the different objects could be put in, in script lettering, and the children should become familiar with the look of the word God, and the name Jesus. With the older children it will be possible to write on the blackboard short sentences such as, "Jesus loves me", "God is love". And it is always a good thing to let the children see the names of the special days written up, such as Easter Day, and Christmas Day.

Everyone who teaches little children will need to use a blackboard, and should be familiar with and, if possible, possess a copy of *Blackboard Self-teaching for Teachers*, by Vera Peake.

MODELS AND MODEL-MAKING. Children over five still like to see things "in bulk", and can generally get a much better idea of unfamiliar objects from a model than they can from a flat picture. It is the normal thing for a Kindergarten to be provided with models for the use of the teachers. But this is not always the case, and it may happen that teachers will have to make their own. These will be needed chiefly for illustrating Bible stories, to explain the eastern customs; and also for missionary stories. Instructions for making the former can be found in *Biblical Models and how to make them*, Evans and Walker, from the National Society and S.P.C.K. Instructions for making missionary models can be obtained from the various Missionary Societies.

But many people have a natural gift for making models of anything they have seen or of which they have seen a copy, and could, for example, make a simple but very beautiful Stable out of a small wooden or cardboard box, with figures made from pictures pasted on to plywood, or cardboard, and cut out. With a little ingenuity many useful models can be made from such things as matchboxes, empty cotton reels, clothes pegs, pipe-cleaners, corks, beads, etc. Instructions for using the first of these can be found in *Palestine Models: Make your own from Matchboxes*; and *Bible Buildings: Matchboxes—make them into Models*; both by John Elphinstone-Fyffe and published by The Church Information Board.

Models can also be made from clay or plasticine, either alone or combined with some of the things mentioned above. A Galilean fishing-boat could be made from plasticine, with a pencil or a wooden skewer for the mast, and a sail cut from a piece of brown cotton material. A hair-net makes a very good fishing-net, and fish can be cut from silver paper or cellophane. The sea could be represented by light blue material or soft paper arranged in folds, and a small doll's clothes peg could be dressed for the fisherman.

A sheep-fold can be made from cardboard, roughened with clay or plasticine, the shepherd from a peg, and sheep from pipe-cleaners. Round huts for a native village can be made from pieces of corrugated cardboard and roofed with thick, coarse string frayed to look like thatch; the inhabitants could be made with brown plasticine.

But it is not only the teacher who can make models; the children are all eager to make something, and a lesson can very usefully be followed up by letting them make some of the things that have come into the story. For this they can use clay, plasticine, or paper; the paper will probably have to be prepared beforehand by the teacher. For example, they could make palm trees to put in a sand tray by rolling broad strips of brown paper into small tubes and sticking into the top a bunch of thin strips previously cut from crinkled green paper. The trunk of the tree can be fastened with the help of the teacher, either with paste, or by twisting round it a small rubber band, or with a paper fastener at each end.

With clay and plasticine the children will need little help as they have a natural gift for handling soft, responsive material, and can often give to their handiwork a remarkable impression of life and movement. A little girl of six made a plasticine model of a mother washing her little girl's hair, and one could almost see the familiar movements of the mother's hands, and the squirming of the child!

FLANNELGRAPH. This method, useful for all age-groups, is particularly suitable for Kindergarten children. It has some of the advantages of the two previous methods : pictures can be built up as the lesson progresses, and children can handle the cut-outs and move them about on the flannel-board. For this a blackboard, piece of plywood, or very firm cardboard is required. A Radio or T.V. set packing case makes a very convenient board which can be folded up and carried easily. On this is mounted a background of fluffy material such as flannelette or winceyette, dyed black, dark blue, or green. Other suitable materials are lint, domett, or filter cloth. Figures for building up Biblical scenes and Church services are provided in the *Flannel Board Cut-out Books, Nos. 1-4*, from S.P.C.K. and other sources. The cut-outs should be coloured and backed with similar material to that on the board. They will then adhere to the background wherever they are placed, and the story can be illustrated graphically by building up the scenes and making the characters move.

In the same way frieze pictures can be made, or other stories illustrated, the figures being cut from pictures, magazines, etc., or in silhouette from stiff coloured paper, as required.

CHAPTER 14

METHODS OF TEACHING THE KINDERGARTEN CHILD—II

LEARNING BY HEART. The Kindergarten child is beginning to grow away from the jingle of nursery rhymes, and is becoming more able to learn by heart intelligently. But he needs a good deal of help, not only with the understanding of the words, but in the committing of them to memory. This help can best be given by telling him a story about the hymn, psalm, or poem, and by using in the story, as far as possible, the actual words to be learnt. It will be found that by the end of the story the words are already half known, and a little repetition will enable him to get the whole thing by heart in a very short time.

This method can very well be used for teaching the first two verses of the hymn, *All things bright and beautiful,* instead of the blackboard method which could be reserved for the remaining verses, to be taught later on. During the week before the lesson the teacher should go for a walk in the country and collect specimens of as many bright and beautiful things as possible : flowers, leaves, moss, fir-cones, berries, etc., according to the season, and perhaps some feathers and a few attractive pebbles. These should be taken to the class, together with some pictures of birds, insects, and animals. If no suitable pictures are available, blackboard sketches would be helpful. The lesson would be introduced by a talk on what we see when we walk to school, and the lesson itself would describe a walk in the country, and what we saw as we went along. The walk should be adapted from the one taken by the teacher in the week, so that the descriptions can be as vivid as possible. Throughout the lesson the words of the hymn would be used, and at each point the appropriate object or picture shown : all creatures great and small would be illustrated with pictures, which could also be used for each little bird that sings; but for all things bright and beautiful, all things wise and wonderful, and each little flower that opens, the various objects would be used. As each teacher would describe a familiar walk it is only possible to make suggestions here. They are real incidents selected from several short walks taken with two little girls during a spring holiday in Sussex, and pieced together to make a story.

After getting the children to talk about what they saw on the way to school, the Introduction would end like this : Now I will tell you about the lovely walk I had on Easter Monday with my two little nieces, and the beautiful things we saw.

1. THE PATH THROUGH THE MEADOW

(*a*) *All things bright and beautiful.* First of all we crossed the stile just beyond the bus stop, and followed the path by the side of the meadow. Everything looked so bright and beautiful : the grass was getting green again after the long winter, in the hedges we found lots of beautiful things—pussy willow and lambs' tails, and there were bright, pinky specks of buds on the branches (show any specimens collected). And just see these tiny stones we found (show) : they are bright and beautiful things, too, though we do not often notice them. All things bright and beautiful are precious things.

(*b*) *All creatures great and small.* Then we heard a rustling on the other side of the hedge. "Bulls!" screamed one of the little girls, and we saw the head of a great creature poking through a gap. He certainly looked very big, and the children were all for running back to the road; but soon we were able to see that he was really quite young, only a rather big calf (show picture). There were several calves in that field, and both children were glad when we had crossed a second stile into a lane.

Here there were trees on both sides, and suddenly a grey squirrel slipped out of one of them, ran across the lane, and up into another tree. We only just caught a glimpse of him : he looked a very small creature after the great calves, and *he* was afraid of *us* and scampered away as fast as he could go. The children would have liked to stroke him, but he was gone (show picture).

It was very warm in the lane and we actually saw gnats darting about under the trees. They were such very small creatures, and moved so quickly, that we really could not see what they were like.

All these creatures we saw, great and small—calves, the squirrel, and the gnats—they all seemed to be so glad that spring had come.

2. THE CHURCHYARD

(a) *All things wise and wonderful.* We came to a Church and went into the churchyard through the front gate. The first thing we saw was a very old yew tree. It is so large that, if we had all joined hands, we could not have reached round it. Its trunk is all twisted and hollow, and it hardly seems possible that it can still be alive. But it is, for the branches are thick with dark, spiky leaves (show a piece of yew). It is a very wonderful old tree and I am sure that it is very wise, too. It must know such a lot of things for it has stood there, near the Church door, for hundreds of years ! But it is getting tired now, and its heavy branches are all propped up with stakes to keep them off the ground.

What do you think we saw on one of those branches, just where the prop was supporting it ? Something else very wise and wonderful (let children have one or two guesses). Some birds had built their nest there and the mother bird was actually sitting on it ! (Show a nest, or some model eggs.)

She was only a little higher than my head, but she did not move a feather when we peeped at her. She looked so wise, one bright eye watching us while she guarded her eggs; wise and wonderful, because her nest was so beautifully made, and she had chosen such a safe place for it. So the little girls and I tip-toed by, so that we might not disturb her, and went on into the Church.

(b) *The Lord God made them all.* How bright and beautiful the Church looked, with the Easter flowers still fresh. We knelt down for a few moments to say "Thank you" to the Lord God, our Heavenly Father, for all things bright and beautiful, all creatures great and small—the great calves, the small squirrel, the tiny gnats; all things wise and wonderful—the wise old tree, the wonderful bird on her nest. For the Lord God made them all.

3. THE WOODS

(a) *Each little flower that opens.* We came home through some lovely woods, full of flowers: masses of primroses, great clumps of them. Some of the little flowers were only just opening, and there were such a lot of buds (show any flowers that have been brought). The two girls had never seen primroses growing in a wood before, and they picked a great bunch of them to take home. Then we saw some violets, great patches of glowing colour among the pale yellow primroses. Just as we were leaving we found one or two bluebells beginning to come up. We did not need to go back into the Church to say another "Thank you" to the Lord God for each little flower that opens. We know that he made their glowing colours, just as he made all things bright and beautiful.

(b) *Each little bird that sings.* As we left the woods the birds were beginning to sing their evening hymn. There must have been hundreds of them in the trees, almost every kind of little bird that sings. Some of them fluttered about so close to us that we could see the feathers in their tiny wings (show some feathers, or a picture). So we said "Thank you" again to our Heavenly Father, for each little flower that opens, each little bird that sings. He made their glowing colours, he made their tiny wings. The Lord God made them all.

For the Conclusion, tell the children that there is a hymn in our book that talks about all the bright and beautiful things that you saw on your walk.

Read or, if practicable, sing the first two verses of the hymn, showing each article or picture in turn, as you come to them. Then get the children to sing or say the verses with you. After a time or two let them try it alone, helping them where necessary. It should not be long before they can all manage it together.

In the closing worship an attempt should be made to sing the two verses which have been learnt. This should be followed by a well-known thanksgiving hymn, such as *"Thank you!" for the world so sweet*, or *Thank him, thank him, all ye little children*.

Some hymns lend themselves to this kind of treatment, but there are others for which neither this, nor the blackboard method already described, would be suitable. When no other way is possible, hymns, poems, and psalms can be taught by repetition only, after a story about them has been told. But it is important that a whole verse should be repeated each time, not line by line or only a few meaningless words at a time. With an eight-line verse it may be possible to take four lines together, provided they make sense. After hearing a verse a few times the children will be able to sing or say it over with the teacher, and then alone. The following week it will probably be found that they are able to repeat it right through with very little help.

As these children cannot read easily it is very necessary for them to know a fair number of hymns by heart, and teachers should not be content for them to sing a few over and over again. Especially should they learn hymns and verses of praise, so that they can store up in their minds acts of praise that can be used on all occasions.

DRAMATIZATION. Reference has already been made to *Activity*, or *Things to do*, with an insistence that it must be some form of self-expression, that is, expression of something that is part of oneself. If a lesson has been well given, and well received, it will have become part of the make-up of the mind of the child, and so it will be possible for the child to give some form of expression to it, while at the same time the very act of giving expression to it will greatly strengthen the impression that has been made.

In the Nursery School the tiny children, who have little apparent purpose in their activities, are left to express themselves very much as the spirit moves them, with little more than suggestions from the teacher, often in the form of music. In the Kindergarten it is possible to relate the self-expression much more closely to the main point of the lesson, because of the new element of purpose in the children's activities. This means that the teacher will generally plan beforehand what form the activity shall take, although he will always allow some freedom of choice.

In making these plans the teacher must consider two things : (1) that the activity shall meet the characteristic needs of the children, and (2) that it must be suitable to the lesson subject. These two rules hold good whatever the age of the children we teach.

Several forms of activity have already been considered : drawing, sand-trays, paper-modelling, making things, learning by heart, etc. One of the most successful forms of self-expression for children in the Kindergarten and Junior age-groups is Dramatization, that is, acting a story that has been told. With the little ones this can be practically spontaneous, and can be wordless miming, or with just the main characters speaking the few most important words. In the story of Blind Bartimæus, one of the suggested *Things to do* is, Act the story. This the children could do with very little help from the teacher. One child would be chosen for the blind man, and others for the disciples, while the crowd would have to be imagined (unless the acting were a combined effort of the whole school, when there would be enough children for the crowd as well). The words of our Lord should be repeated by the teacher, and Bartimæus and one or two of the disciples could speak. It would not be necessary for them to learn the words, as they could say what they remembered of the *meaning* in their own words. In this way they would really be expressing what the lesson had meant to them.

Since the acting is to express what the story means to the children, we must be quite sure that it has, in fact, some meaning for them. In other words, no attempt should be made to act a story unless the teacher is satisfied that the story which has been told is both *known* and *understood*. It is quite possible for children to look as though they are taking in every word when, as a few well-chosen questions will reveal, they have not really been listening at all. Some teachers have found it more satisfactory to have a story, followed by drawing, one week; and then to revise the story the following week to make sure that it is really known, after which the story can be acted. If a lesson book is being used, this will mean dropping out one of the other lessons, but it is worth while doing this to ensure that the acting is of real value to the children.

If the classes are all held in one large room it may not be possible to get much movement into the acting, but within the circle of chairs that forms the class it should be possible for six or eight children to do something in the way of re-enacting the scene. If the class is in a separate room the reproduction can be more elaborate, and one part of the room will be arranged to represent the city gate through which the crowd will pass.

With small children, when parts have to be chosen, this should be done by the teacher. Older children can be allowed to choose, not their own parts, but who shall represent the various characters.

It is also possible to dramatize a story on a miniature stage, and this has been done very successfully with the story of the Breakfast on the Seashore (John 21. 1-14). A blue cloth was arranged on the floor at the side of the room, to represent the sea of Galilee and alongside, in a half circle, sawdust was spread to look like a beach. Against the wall was a frieze of hills, and on the sea were one or two small boats. A little fire of twigs was arranged on the beach, lit by a small electric bulb under red paper, and round it, on some stones, were placed a few tiny silver fish and some small biscuits for loaves. The whole scene was covered until after the story had been told, when the children were asked if they would like to come and have breakfast with the friends of the Lord Jesus, and they gathered by the seashore. One of them was allowed to hand round the biscuits, which they all ate very reverently after grace had been said. They entered so very really into the spirit of the scene that the teacher said afterwards she felt they had been given a foretaste of Communion.

Something like this might be done in a room shared with other classes, where it would not be possible to act the whole story in detail. The scene could be arranged beforehand against the wall behind the circle of chairs, and covered up or screened off until required; or prepared in a large sand-tray and kept covered until the story was ended, and then put on the floor within the circle, with the children grouped at one side.

Teachers should read, *Making Bible Plays for Little Ones*, by F. Collins, published by A. R. Mowbray & Co., Ltd.

OTHER METHODS. Some of the methods used in the Nursery School can still be used in the Kindergarten, though in a modified form. As seen above, there is a place for the sand-tray, but it will generally be kept in reserve until the end of the lesson. It may sometimes be better to let each child have a small tray in which he can work out his own designs, giving scope for his creative powers.

Pictures will also be used, and they should be large and clear, with good strong colours, but they can now contain more detail, and the children can be asked more thoughtful questions about them. Instead of saying, "Show me the little boy Jacky", we can now say, "What do you think Jacky is going to do?"

It is better not to let the children handle the pictures, but they should be held close enough for the children to see and touch, so that they can ask any questions they like about them.

Pictures can be used at the beginning of a lesson to recall a previous lesson; to attract attention and arouse interest; and to get the right set of ideas into the children's minds before beginning the lesson proper. They can be used at any time during a lesson to illustrate some particular point, such as the kind of house in which the Lord Jesus lived; to recall wandering attention; or to introduce a new section of the lesson. And they can be used at the end of a lesson to impress the main point of the lesson on the minds of the children, to revise the whole lesson by asking them questions about the picture, or to give an illustration of something else similar to the subject of the lesson.

Sometimes a whole lesson can be built up around a series of pictures, such as stories of children, leading up to the story of the Baby Jesus. For this there could be a picture of the Baby Moses, the Infant Samuel, and perhaps one of John the Baptist as a little boy. Last of all there would be a picture of the Madonna and Child. These would be shown in turn, and the story of each told so as to show how precious each child was, and how the Heavenly Father took care of each one of them. Or there could be a series of pictures of Friends of Jesus, showing Jesus Blessing the Children; Calling his Disciples; Teaching the People; Talking to Mary of Bethany. This is a very good way of introducing the children to the characters in the Gospel story.

Music will play an important part in the Kindergarten programme but, as this will be part of the organization of the whole Department, it will be in the hands of the Superintendent. Eurythmics and Ring Games can be used, and there should be a period of free play, for which suitable apparatus—picture-books, drawing and painting materials, clay or plasticine, etc.—should be provided.

CHAPTER 15

CHARACTERISTICS OF CHILDREN
AGED SEVEN TO ELEVEN YEARS

WE NOW have to consider the characteristics of the Junior Child, and he is not nearly so easy a subject for consideration as the younger child because he is going through a period of considerable growth and development—physical, mental, and moral. During the greater part of this time the child is gradually passing from childhood into boyhood or girlhood, and the passage is not usually a steady, orderly progress. It is rather like that of the snail climbing a wall, who was said to advance by going up two inches and dropping back one. In the boy or girl at this age there is often much of the Kindergarten Child, while at the same time there is a definite reaching out towards the fuller development of the older child. This does not mean that the Junior Child is neither one thing nor the other; he is a very real personality with his own characteristic behaviour, but it does mean that there is very often a tension within that growing personality which makes his behaviour appear to be inconsistent. This tension is due to the presence of a very strong urge to press forward and experience all that life can offer, and a very natural reluctance to relinquish all the security and well-tried delights of childhood. This tension is a very valuable part of the child's development, although at the time it may seem to have many disadvantages. Without this urge forward the child who has had a happy, sheltered childhood might very well prefer to stay as he is, and would perhaps never learn to be independent and self-reliant. If, on the other hand, he felt no reluctance he might break away entirely from all control, and so lose the guidance and protection of those older and more experienced than himself, of which he is still very much in need. Once we have understood the reason for this tension the apparent inconsistency of his behaviour disappears.

A child of this age will have gone up into a new Day School Department and, conscious of his new dignity, he may consider himself too grown-up to play with the younger children at home. If so he will keep aloof and perhaps try to settle down to read a real boys' book. But reading may not yet be very easy for him, and it needs a good deal of effort to concentrate while an exciting game of make-believe is going on. Only a few weeks ago he would have been the chief figure in such a game, and it is difficult to accept the fact that it can be played successfully without him. So he watches out of the corner of his eye and, when at last the game shows signs of flagging for lack of leadership, he can resist no longer. All the child in him yearns to take his old place again and, having given up the struggle, his surrender will be complete and he will give himself up to the game as thoroughly as he has always done in the past.

The same kind of tension is present in his many other activities. His growing powers of mind and limb give him a new self-confidence and independence, and he will often be too venturesome, or undertake tasks beyond his ability. At such times he is, in his own estimation, monarch of all he surveys. But his plans often miscarry : his adventure ends in a fall, and a badly cut knee; his skill does not come up to his expectations; or he finds that he has unwittingly aroused the wrath of a grown-up of whom he had expected better things. Then, because he still retains much of the younger child's trustfulness, his world comes tumbling down like a house of cards, and he needs the loving sympathy of those to whom be has always turned for help when in trouble.

The story of *Alice in Wonderland*, by Lewis Carroll, illustrates very well indeed this state of tension in which the Junior Child so often finds himself—now too big, now too small to cope with the situations with which life presents him. He is so seldom just the right size, and it will only be when he has come to the full stature of boyhood that, like Alice, he will be able to say to his fears and perplexities: " 'Who cares for you?' . . . (she had grown to her full size by this time). 'You're nothing but a pack of cards!' "

If the adult understands these two needs of the Junior Child—reasonable freedom to experiment with the new powers of which he is conscious, and comfort or encouragement when he is overwhelmed with disaster, or stricken with a sense of failure—then the adult will be able to help him successfully through this rather difficult period. Two things must always be avoided. We must never treat him as a baby, however babyish his behaviour may be, unless he himself desires it because of some real need. Then he should be given the comfort that he seeks. Moreover, we must never tease him, either for being a baby or for putting on grown-up airs. If we do, we shall lose his trust and with it all chance of being able to help him when he most needs us. The best way to help a child out of babyish ways is, with quiet confidence, to treat him as an older child.

We must now try to describe the characteristic behaviour of this rapidly developing child, but it cannot be done so neatly as that of the young child because of the apparent contradictions, and also because he displays different characteristics when alone from those which come into play when with other children, and again when with adults. But there are two main, outstanding characteristics of this age, the first of which profoundly affects his behaviour in all circumstances, and these are: (1) *eagerness*, (2) *a corporate spirit*.

1. This characteristic *eagerness* is shown in all the child's responses to life, and can most conveniently be considered under the three headings of physical, mental, and moral development.

(*a*) Physically, his *energy* seems to be boundless and he throws himself into whatever he is doing with a zest which often appears out of all proportion to the object of his zeal. If he is asked to take a simple and quite unimportant message, he will tear off to deliver it as if the welfare of the whole household depended upon its immediate delivery. He is always eager to help, and when given a task is often so anxious to accomplish it that he does not wait to do it thoroughly. Almost before the echo of his footsteps has died away he is back again, asking what he can do now. If he is not kept well supplied with jobs, and allowed to expend un- limited energy on them, he will soon lose interest and go off to find more congenial occupations. But suitable jobs are not always easy to find, and one can sympathize with a father who, in desperation, sent his small son to the railway station, some twenty minutes' walk away, to deposit a suitcase in the cloakroom, and sent him again later in the day to recover it! The child can quite well find occupations for himself, and should be encouraged to do so. But the young child in him will want our attention, and he will come again and again to show us what he is doing, and seek approval. We must recognize this need and meet it with sympathy and patience.

In all his games and occupations the child shows the same energy, and when walking with adults often covers the ground three times by running on ahead and then back again to examine something he had noticed on the way. Even so his energy is not exhausted, and is always ready to be diverted into other channels. One such outlet is provided by his *pugnacity*, for the Junior Child is ever ready to have a scrap. Usually this takes the form of a friendly tussle, but sometimes he fights in self-defence, often with a boy much bigger than himself, and occasionally, in a fit of rage, he will attack an adult. The more usual friendly scrap will start suddenly without apparent cause, and as suddenly cease, and would appear to be nothing more than an urgent need to make use of the fists.

At this age his activities have a much more definite plan and purpose than with the younger child, and he is able to perform difficult feats with surprising *agility*. One boy at this age made a clever and complicated run for his scooter by arranging some single planks in a long, straight line, but at varying levels, to make a kind of switch-back. The boards were placed across boxes, etc., of different heights, the highest being about two feet from the ground, and in the middle of the run he placed the garden roller so that a board rested on it and then reached to the end of the handle, upon which it was exactly balanced. Below it was another plank, about a foot lower, and when the boy on the scooter approached the extremity of the upper board the handle was weighed down and allowed him to pass with a bump, but without a break, along the lower plank to the end of the run. It looked horribly dangerous, but the boy was fearless and never had a spill. Boys and girls at this age will climb anything that can be climbed, and will go far up into trees that would daunt an older child.

But his activities are not all violent, for he is capable of skilful operations that require little energy. He is beginning to show considerable *constructional ability*, and will build the most complicated railway systems which, if permitted by the rest of the household, will permanently cover the whole floor of a room. He is not so content as he was to make "something out of anything," for he is much more critical of his handiwork and often dissatisfied with the results of his efforts. But at this age both boys and girls are usually keenly interested in constructional toys such as

Meccano, and the many kinds of wooden, plastic, or metal sectional toys that can be built up into houses, cars, or planes. Many girls at this age are quite skilful with needle and thread, and will often insist on making their own presents for their friends and relations.

(b) Mentally, the Junior child's eagerness is shown in many ways. His *curiosity* has developed into an eagerness to learn and a thirst for detail. This is the reason for his perpetual question, "Why?" and he is no longer satisfied with a simple answer, but insists upon a full explanation. He will also carry out investigations himself, especially in connection with insects and caterpillars, and often seems to be cruel in his methods; yet he is not intentionally cruel, but longing to satisfy his eager curiosity. He begins to become critical of the knowledge and sincerity of the grown-ups to whom he directs his questions. The desire for information and passion for investigation are valuable aids to his education, for some of his physical energy can be transformed into mental energy by setting him to work to discover the answers to his own questions.

In this he is helped by a new quality in his *imagination*, which is becoming much more dependent on facts. The world of make-believe is gradually slipping away and the child is becoming intensely interested in the real world around and beyond him. But in order to make a true mental picture of things outside his actual experience he must have all the available facts. When these are supplied he can get to work on them as industriously as bees on wax, and he will be able to give an extraordinarily complete, if not always quite accurate, account of something that he has never seen.

The things that he learns at this age he will probably always remember, for he now has a *quick and retentive memory*. The problem is no longer how to get him to learn by heart, but how to supply him with material that is worth being committed to memory. It was once discovered that a boy who had never shown any great enthusiasm for going to Church knew a number of hymns by heart, and among them some of the most worthy of our fine collection of English hymns. When asked how he came to know them so well, he explained that sermons always bored him and so he spent the sermon time in Church selecting, and committing to memory, the hymns that appealed to him. The Junior Child does not only remember things that can be learnt by heart; all the facts which he is continually discovering are being stored up on the shelves of his mental library, about which we were thinking in an earlier chapter, and this is the time when he should be trained to arrange these stored-up facts in an orderly manner.

Perhaps one of the best ways to help him to do this is by a sympathetic attitude towards his *acquisitiveness*, that passion for collecting anything and everything, whether of value or not, which is so marked at this age. He will, as we have seen, collect information of all kinds, including such things as the different makes of motor-car or plane, which he can usually recognize at a glance. He also collects all sorts of odds and ends—corks, string, acorns, shells, screws, etc.—as the turning out of any boy's pocket or girl's drawer will show. This indiscriminate collecting can, with a little encouragement, be guided along the lines of a more orderly collection of definite things such at wild flowers, stamps, and newspaper photographs. These he can be helped to arrange carefully, and by so doing his mind will be indirectly trained in the orderly arrangement of information. One other thing he can be trained to collect, and that is good habits. If he is helped to see why a habit is a good one he will adopt it as eagerly as any of the other facts in which he is interested.

He is rapidly becoming a reasonable being, and is developing a *reasoning power* that will be of extreme value to him if rightly directed. A child of 7, paddling in the sea, was asked to get her bucket from the place on the beach where she and her brother had been digging. She returned with both buckets saying, "I thought if I left one by itself someone might think it was left behind, and take it." The Junior Child can follow up a simple line of thought, so long as it is not argumentative, and is able to form judgements which, although sometimes unsound, are none the less based on reason. His lack of actual experience often makes it impossible for his judgements always to be wise, and later on he will of his own accord revise many of them. In our teaching we can make use of this reasoning power in the working out of lessons, and the building up of summaries which should be the result of the child's own thinking. He will be able to appreciate the value of the Creeds as summaries of the Church's teaching, and this again will encourage him to commit them to memory.

(c) Morally, the eagerness of the Junior child is also very marked. He is beginning to have a very definite *sense of right and wrong*, although at this stage it is more often exercised in connection with other people's failure to keep the rules than with his own, which he does not very readily admit. Perhaps this is as well, as he might otherwise be overwhelmed with a sense of his own failure. One of the rather difficult things about the child of this age is the tendency to tell tales, which is due to an eager desire that the right thing should be done and, if it has not been done, that the matter should be put right. This accounts for his coming to the person who is able to deal with the situation and put the matter right. But although he seems more concerned with the wrong behaviour of other people, he can very well understand when he himself has done what is wrong, and experience a very real need of forgiveness. This is very important, for our Christian faith is a religion of forgiveness, and so soon as a child can begin to understand something of its meaning it is time for him to be taught about sin and forgiveness and the sacramental means of grace. It is not only foolish, but definitely wrong, to allow a child to think he has fulfilled all his obligations in the way of apology when he has flung a light-hearted "Sorry" over his shoulder.

Along with this growing sense of right and wrong there is an eager *love of truth*. No longer is the child satisfied with the mere delight in a story; his first question will most probably be "Is it true?" and if the answer is "No", then it is made very clear that there is no market for our wares. This might cut out many valuable stories, such as the parables of our Lord, if it were not possible to help the child to see that there can be an inner truth which is every bit as important as a story which is true in fact. This can be done by likening the setting of the parable to the shell of a nut, of which the kernel resembles the inner truth of the story. The shell is important because it holds the nut and protects it, and in much the same way the parable, or allegory, holds and protects the truth. This love of truth often makes the child disconcertingly frank, but it is quite simply a sincerity which he has not yet learnt to temper with tact. We should appreciate this and bear with him patiently. A father was taking his small son, aged 7, to join his mother and two younger sisters who had been staying for ten days with an aunt. As they set out he said, "Won't it be lovely to see Mummy and the girls again?" But the boy replied, "*I* want to see Auntie Catherine".

The Junior Child is now entering on a career of *hero-worship* that may carry him well into adult life, though the type of hero that appeals to him will change with the changes in himself. At this stage a man is a hero first for what he *does*, and he must do great things or cease to be a hero. Once accepted as a hero, he will also be admired for what he *is*. National or international champions of any kind hold first place, especially in such matters as cricket and football, in which the child can be a humble follower. Then there are such lesser lights as the clown at the circus and the leader of the nigger minstrels on the sands. There are more remote heroes such as dirt-track racers, or long-distance pilots; and films, radio, and television provide a wide range of choice either of stars, or the characters they impersonate. But the favourites are always those who do on a grand scale the things that the child is able to do in his own modest way, because he can then more easily imagine that he is the hero himself, and this gives him very great satisfaction. This capacity for hero-worship gives us our opportunity for introducing him to the heroes of the Church, and among these we can, as we have already seen, include many of the Old Testament characters, so long as we select those who gave themselves to the service of God.

These can all be presented to him as models truly worthy of his study, for by now his love of *imitation* has changed from a gift for mimicry into an eager desire to be like the person admired, both by doing the things that he does and also by displaying the qualities that he displays in doing them. So we can use this passion for imitating the character-istics of the hero by encouraging the child to admire the noble qualities of the saints of God.

Where the child admires he also trusts, and one of the most precious characteristics of the child of this age is his *trust in God*, which can be a very real experience provided he has had full opportunities of forming this relationship. The world is still wonderful to him, and behind it all is God, and nothing is too wonderful for Him to do. Yet it is not a blind, unreasoning trust. The question arose as to whether the story of the golden image, *Daniel* 3, were a true one. A boy of 8 ended the discussion by saying, "You know, I think it is true. God does do things like that—look at Moses." A boy of 10 once said, "God always gives me everything I ask for", and then added, "Of course, I don't worry Him about unimportant things." This trust must be carefully cherished, and the child helped to realize that prayer is always answered, even when the answer is not "Yes".

2. So far we have been considering the Junior Child as an individual, but the child of this age is not normally individualistic. Though there may be times when he likes to be alone, he is usually at his happiest in a group of children of his own age. He is developing a very definite *corporate spirit*, and is now able to play with other children in the real sense of doing things together. For some time this will take the form of doing the same thing that the others are doing, and often this seems to be more important than the actual thing that is being done. Usually one of them will be the leader and the rest will eagerly follow him, some perhaps without being aware why they are doing it. This explains the popularity of the game, Follow my leader, in which they all closely follow the lead of one child and copy every gesture. In many of their games the favourite method of progress is by following one after the other in single file. In this way they run together and stop together : if they are pretending to be soldiers and one of them shoots at an imaginary enemy, they all immediately put rifle to shoulder and shoot; if one should run up some steps and jump down again, they will all do it. Sometimes they seem to have discovered the secret of perpetual motion : a group of children was playing in a barn half-filled with hay, part of which was still firmly stacked while the rest was loosely piled on the ground waiting to be carted away. The children ceaselessly climbed up on to the firm hay, and then jumped into the soft hay below, one after the other, only to climb up again and again jump until it seemed that nothing but sheer exhaustion would ever stop them! The same kind of thing can be seen wherever there are similar opportunities, such as sand heaps, piles of stones, or a fixed seat in a park. During a Sunday School Christmas Party the superintendent went

into the room where the Juniors were playing. She found a very worried-looking teacher standing helplessly in the middle of the room, note-book in hand, while the children ran about or leapt from the benches round the wall. When asked how she was getting on she said, "They are supposed to be having a team game, according to the programme, but I cannot get any of them to play it". It was suggested that as it was, after all, the children's party, it was a pity to try to make them do something they would not enjoy. So a pianist was found, and a mat placed on the floor, and they were soon rushing round playing "musical mat" at top speed, thoroughly happy. The rules were not very strictly kept, and children who were "out" generally came "in" again; but it served to use up a good deal of their energy so that they were ready to settle to something quieter later on.

Team games are not very attractive at this age because the children have not yet become co-operative and are not very interested in sides. They do play such organized games as cricket and netball, but they are usually more concerned with their own score than with the question of which side is winning. We can see from this that if we want to get corporate work from Junior children we must get them all to work on the same task, but having achieved this we can then encourage them all to do their best by introducing a little competition into the activity.

Those who would like to make a fuller study of the Junior Child should read, *The Junior Sunday School*, by C. R. Newby, revised by L. M. Naylor, and published by the National Society and S.P.C.K.

CHAPTER 16

ONE of the best ways of getting the children to work together corporately is by letting them do some form of handwork. At one time there was a good deal of prejudice against letting children do things with their hands in Sunday School, either from an idea that it was wrong to do things on Sunday, or from an unwillingness to introduce Day School methods. One elderly teacher, when asked to let her little girls of seven do some drawing, answered, "No, they are too young, it is better for them to sit still and listen." But from what we now know of the seven-year-old we can understand that this was just what those little girls could not do. Their awe of the teacher helped them to sit still for quite a long time, but it is very doubtful if they did much listening. When children's bodies cannot be active their minds will be, but they generally go off on their own mental adventures when asked to listen too long to someone else who is doing all the talking. If we can provide some activity for their bodies we shall find that their minds will be much less restless, and so handwork can be a real help to both teacher and children.

But handwork is not merely a device for keeping children occupied and out of mischief; it has a definite value of its own and, if rightly used, can become a practical means of helping the development of the fruit of the Spirit, that harvest of the Christian character which James Moffatt has translated as *love, joy, peace, good temper, kindliness, generosity, fidelity, gentleness, self-control* (Galatians 5.

22-23). As children work together there is a gradual deepening of the sense of fellowship, which is the corporate expression of love; there is the joy of achievement shared together; their unity in a common purpose will make for peace among them; the children begin to learn that to be good-tempered in the acceptance of difficulties is the best preparation for overcoming them; kindliness is encouraged when a more successful child lags behind in order to help a less skilful child; generosity is called for in the sharing of a common store of materials; the children discover the need for accuracy in the making of models and so learn the value of fidelity in the carrying out of a task; in handling delicate pieces of work they will realize that gentleness is a necessity; and in learning to control the various materials they are using, the children are also being trained in self-control.

These are only beginnings, for the lessons go on being learnt all through life; but the first steps in any direction are the most important as they set the course for the whole journey. The lessons are also being learnt unconsciously, and we must not make any attempt to point the moral; but use can be made of the experience gained to illustrate future lessons as, for example, a lesson on the value of truth, when the teacher can say, "Do you remember that when you were making that model of an eastern house each little piece had to be exactly true?"

While having a value of its own, handwork in religious education is not an end in itself; it should be closely related to the instruction that is being given. It has often been said that there is no *impression* without *expression*, and although this may not be strictly true, it can safely be said that the surest way to make an impression permanent is to provide opportunity for giving it some form of outward expression. A child of seven who had just come home from Sunday School was asked what the lesson had been, and could not remember anything about it. The child's mother explained that the children had a new teacher who did not let them draw, and so they had nothing to help them to remember the lesson. Handwork can often serve this purpose most successfully, but it should be regarded as only one of many useful forms of self-expression. For many types of lesson it would be quite unsuitable, but when it is possible to use it, the objects to be made should help the children to give practical expression to whatever it has been the aim of the lesson to teach. For instance, a lesson on Helping Others could be followed by the making of models that were needed in the Kindergarten or Nursery School.

It is often not possible for a teacher to provide any very elaborate handwork for the children to do at the actual lesson time; but in many parishes there is some form of Children's Club where the children meet in the week, and it is a very good plan for the teacher to be in close touch with those in charge of it, and to take some active part in its organization. It would then be possible for suggestions made, and work commenced, on Sunday to be carried out and completed during the week. For class work the easiest form of handwork is making things from paper or thin cardboard. Books can be made from sheets of coloured or brown paper, and poems, prayers, or short stories written in them. These can then be illustrated by the pasting in of pictures cut from illustrated magazines or Christmas cards. The collecting of these pictures and their careful arrangement will appeal to children at this age. With thin cardboard models can be made of a font, a sheepfold, an eastern house or tomb. These would probably have to be cut out in readiness beforehand, and only the folding done in class; any pasting or gumming might have to be done during the week. There are a number of coloured cut-outs which can be obtained from the National Society and S.P.C.K., including a Christmas Crib, an Easter Garden, and various Missionary Scenes. These can all be made up in a class very successfully.

Other materials that can be used are leather, felt, raffia, beads, matchboxes, and all kinds of oddments such as buttons, corks, shells. Clay and papier mâché can also be used, but are more suitable for use in the Club. Teachers will find helpful suggestions in *Biblical Models*, H. W. Whanslaw, published by the Religious Education Press, and in the matchbox booklets already referred to. Useful cut-outs are *Inside the Church: A Picture book of Church Furniture*; and *A Model Font and Altar*, both by J. Elphinstone-Fyffe and published by The Church Information Board.

CHAPTER 17

METHODS OF TEACHING THE JUNIOR CHILD—I

THE PROJECT METHOD. This method will be dealt with in more detail in Chapter 20, as it can be developed more fully with children over eleven years of age, and the initiative in its development can be taken by the children in a greater degree. But it is necessary to follow up what has been said about handwork with a brief reference to the ways in which work of this kind, which may have to be spread over two or three weeks, can be linked up with a definite project. The word comes from two Latin words meaning *throw* and *in front of*, as one might throw a stone or a ball in front of a dog with the idea of making him go after it. The word is used to describe a piece of work that is undertaken with a definite purpose, which is known and planned beforehand, as if the plan and purpose were *thrown in front*, and the attention of the class concentrated on following up the purpose and carrying out the plan.

One can go for a walk, and roam happily all day without caring very much where one goes or how long it takes. But if one plans a walk to visit a certain beauty spot, or to collect specimens of flowers or leaves, or to discover the source of a river, then one can be said to have a project and the walk will partake of the nature of an expedition.

A project usually takes the form of discovering the answer to some question which has been raised, or of investigating some point in which interest has been aroused, perhaps in the course of a lesson on some other subject. In pursuing the quest the child's inquiring mind will reach out in many directions, and he will engage in a variety of activities. These will range from making rough notes, or drawing maps or charts, to the making of an elaborate model to scale, the production of a play, or a series of visits to places of interest. Whatever form the activity may take, it must not be allowed to become so interesting that either teacher or children lose sight of the project itself. It is the work done in class, and the information gained thereby, which is of permanent value, and the activity is only important as a means to that end.

A suitable project for Juniors would be to find out all that we can about *Our Father's House*. This might arise out of a discussion in class during a lesson which included the story of Jesus in the Temple as a boy of 12. Children may have discovered that the authorized version uses the words, *about my Father's business*, while the revised version has, *in my Father's house*, with a marginal note : *Or* about my Father's business; in the things of my Father. There might not be time for a full discussion as to how our Lord's words could mean such seemingly different things, and the suggestion would be made that the next few lessons could be spent in discovering what our Lord meant by *my Father's house*, and seeing how that can help us to understand what *we* mean when we speak of our Father's house.

So the project could start from there and lead to the discovery that our English word *house* can be used in several different ways : for the actual buildings in which people live or in which particular duties are carried out as, for example, the Houses of Parliament; for a family or dynasty, such as the House of Tudor, the House of Windsor; and for the actual business carried on in a building, or by a family or firm, an example of this being the House of Rothschild. This would provide three lines of investigation under the main heading of *our Father's House* :

(1) *The Parish Church*, which is our Father's House in the parish;

(2) *The Congregation of the Church*, which is the family of God in the parish;

(3) *The Worship of the Church*, which is the business carried on by the family of God in our Father's House.

Activities in connection with (1) might include such things as week-day visits to the parish Church in order to examine the different parts of the building and the Church furniture, and so to understand their purpose; use of the cut-outs referred to in chapters 13 and 14; drawing a plan of the parish Church. In connection with (2) there should certainly be attendance at a Baptismal service, of which some explanation should previously have been given and attention drawn to the reception of the baptized child *into the congregation of Christ's flock*; there should also be attendance at a service when the children can *sit among the congregation* (it can usually be arranged for a few members of a congregation to have one or two children with them during a service, and to help them to find the places in Prayer Book and hymn book, if necessary); making a model font; learning the answers to the first four questions in the Catechism. In connection with (3) an attempt would be made to get regular Church attendance by the children established; each child might be encouraged to make a book of prayers for his own use, including any he may like to copy from the Prayer Book; the answer to the question in the Catechism, *What is thy duty towards God?* should be studied and learnt, special attention being given to the words, *to worship him*.

With Junior children a project should not be carried out over too long a period, six or eight weeks being sufficient. Some lessons could, however, be repeated in a slightly different form.

It is possible to have a project the purpose of which is to make or produce some definite thing, which could be a corporate activity, and it can be of value provided the thing to be made is worth making and will serve some useful purpose. Even so, it should be accompanied by a study of the various parts to be made or produced, in order to gain the fullest possible information about them. For instance, a model to scale of a proposed new Church might be required as a means of encouraging subscriptions to the building fund. If the children undertook to make the model it would become a project, and very much the same ground would be covered in the lesson periods as for section (1) of the project outlined above. The making of the model might lead to a further project, to discover what is the purpose of having a parish Church, and this would cover the same ground as sections (2) and (3).

A less ambitious project might be to learn as much as possible about the work of one of the Missionary Societies in relation to a particular area overseas. This could be associated with the making of a large book, and the collecting and pasting in of pictures of the Gospel stories, to be sent to children in that area. A study could be made of the seasonal feasts and fasts of the Church, in connection with which a calendar might be made to represent the Church's Year.

The chief value of this method is that it enables us to give much fuller teaching on any one subject, and to relate the various aspects of one subject, by keeping the children's interest sustained in the main theme of the course, and thus holding their attention, over several weeks. And the things that they *do* in connection with the lessons ensure that the instruction given will be retained.

Various books of projects for Junior children can be obtained from the National Society and S.P.C.K.

THE RESEARCH METHOD. This method can be used as a part of a project, but it can also be employed with a single lesson. We have seen that the children of Junior age have an eager curiosity, with a passion for detail, and that they have a great thirst for facts. Their questions sometimes follow each other in such quick succession that they only half-grasp the answers, with the result that they forget a good deal of what they are told, and get some of their information confused. Their speed can be considerably slowed down, and their grasp of the knowledge acquired very much increased, if they are encouraged to seek for the answers to their questions themselves. And we can go farther than this and supply them with suitable questions to which they will be invited to discover the answers. This we can help them to do by means of the research method, in which we shall act as their guides in a voyage of discovery.

In a lesson of this kind we should begin by telling the children what is the problem that they are going to try to solve, and then give them all the material that they will need in their search. This will include Bible references, hymn books, pictures, maps, and any other books of reference that may be required. The problem must be a very simple one, and the children will need a good deal of help from the teacher in the way of explanation and illustration, which may take the form of a story.

A useful problem for children of nine and ten years old might be to discover how the Lord's Prayer came to us. This is not at all generally known, and it is possible for children and even adults to say it regularly and yet have no idea why it is called The Lord's Prayer! The lesson could be one of a course in which the prayer itself would be studied, but the children would be more interested in doing this if they had already learnt what they could *about* it. The lesson would start with an introductory talk about saying prayers: what we best like to say, which we like best of the prayers we say in Church, and the conversation would be led as soon as possible to the use of the Lord's Prayer.

At the beginning of the Presentation stage the children would be told that the prayer occurs in every service that is held in Church, and they would then be invited to look in their Prayer Books at all the well-known services—Holy Communion, Morning and Evening Prayer, and the Baptismal Service—and find the Lord's Prayer in each. The lesson would go on : Ask the children if they know why it is called by this name, and let them turn to Luke 11. 1-4, to discover that the prayer was given by our Lord to his disciples. It is called The Lord's Prayer because our Lord himself gave it to them. Suggest that they would have been surprised if anyone had told them their prayer would be used by millions of people nearly 2,000 years later, all over the world and in hundreds of different languages. To-day we are going to find out how this has come about, and especially to trace from the beginning how the Lord's Prayer has come to us to-day.

The children should be supplied with two maps—one of the journeys of St Paul, and one showing both Italy and Britain. If it is not possible for them each to have these, the teacher should have two that are large enough for all the children to see them easily. Let them find Jerusalem and then look up Acts 1. 8, and read our Lord's last commission to the apostles. Let them note the stages—Jerusalem, Judea and Samaria, the uttermost part of the earth—and then turn to Acts 5. 42 and 8. 1-4, to see how the first two stages were begun. Let children discover for themselves Judea and Samaria on the map. Tell them that wherever the friends of our Lord went preaching the Word, they would also teach the Lord's Prayer to all who became Christians. As the Gospel travelled, so the Lord's Prayer travelled, too. Remind the children of the three stages, and point out that the Prayer has already completed the first two, and we are now going to follow it through the third. Let children look up Acts 11. 19, and then find Antioch on the map, to the

north of the coastline of Syria, and point out that now,
at last, the Prayer has travelled beyond the borders of
Palestine. Here it paused for a little, while the Church at
Antioch grew strong. Read to them, or let them read aloud,
verses 21-26; it will interest them to learn that it was at
Antioch that followers of our Lord were first called
Christians. Now let them pass on to 13. 1-4, and help the
children to realize that this was the first organized Christian
Mission, and that Barnabas and Saul were the very first
Missionaries to be sent out by the Church to work overseas.
Note the words, *They sailed*, and let the children find
Cyprus. Tell children that there is not time, in this lesson, to
follow all the journeyings of Saul (or Paul as he came to be
called), because we have to follow the trail of the Lord's
Prayer, but we will look at three more of the places he
visited. Let children turn to Acts 16. 8-12, and help them to
find Troas, and Philippi in Macedonia, on the map. Draw
attention to the importance of this, the bringing of the
Lord's Prayer into Europe! An even more important step
was taken near the end of St Paul's mission; here the
children should turn to Acts 28. 11-16. Note the words in
verse 14, *and so we came to Rome*. Let the children find
Rome on the map, and explain that this was important because Rome was the very centre of the Roman Empire and
therefore the most important city in the whole world, and so
the Lord's Prayer had now reached the capital city of the
heathen world. Tell the children that many years later Rome
became the centre of the Christian world, and that throughout the whole of the Roman Empire the Lord's Prayer was
being used. But it still had not reached *the uttermost part of
the earth*. Let the children now look at the second map and
see how far Britain is away from Rome. Tell them that only
a part of Britain ever belonged to Rome, and that after a
time they lost even the part that they once had. They were
driven out by heathen people, who also drove away most of

the Christians. These heathen people were called Angles, and it is from them we get the name of our country, England. For many years England was a heathen country, but at last someone came and brought the Lord's Prayer back to our shores.

Then would follow the story of St Gregory and the Slaves. If it is already known to the children they need only be reminded of it, or they can be encouraged to tell it themselves.

Gregory, a monk, saw some slave boys for sale in the market-place of Rome. They were fair-skinned and very beautiful. Gregory asked to what country they belonged, and if they were Christians. On being told that they were Angles, and pagans, he said, "Alas! what a pity . . . for they have an angelic face and should be heirs with the *angels* in heaven." He never forgot them, and later, when he became Bishop of Rome, he sent St Augustine with a band of missionaries to teach the Angles in their own country. St Augustine became the first Archbishop of Canterbury. Let children find Canterbury on the map, and help them to realize the great debt that we owe to St Gregory and St Augustine.

Ever since then the Church in England has been teaching the Lord's Prayer, and she is still teaching it to her children to-day. Let the children repeat, if they know it, the teaching on the Lord's Prayer in the Catechism; if they do not know it, let them find and read it. Help them to realize the wonder of our having such a prayer, coming to us directly from our Lord through the Church. Remind children that the prayer has still not reached all the *uttermost part of the earth*, and that the Church is still sending out missionaries to carry the Prayer to those who do not yet know it.

At the end of the lesson it might be suggested that we could help in this work if we made some books of the Lord's Prayer for missionaries to use when teaching it to children overseas. If the children already support a particular mission, the books could be sent there. They would be made in readiness after this lesson, and completed later. The plan would be to paste on each page a picture illustrating each sentence of the Prayer, and to write it underneath, if possible, in the language of the people to whom the books would be sent.

It can easily be seen that the children would learn far more readily by this method than they would by merely being told about it.

THE USE OF STORIES.   It will be seen from the foregoing that for Juniors a lesson is no longer a story. For one thing, a good many of the stories we may want to use will already be well known, at any rate to some of the children, and they would get impatient if asked to listen to them again. They no longer love repetition as they did when they were very young, and in their eagerness to learn more they would feel it waste of time to listen to what they already knew. "I know that" very often brings a lesson to an untimely end if the teacher is not prepared with something else to use instead of the story. But there is still a place for the story in the teaching of Junior children, and often in one lesson there may be two or three stories. In the lesson given above, the story of Gregory and the Slaves was used as a link to fill in a gap between two pieces of research work. Even if this is not necessary, it is often a good plan to give the children a break from work, and they will be glad to put their books down for a few minutes and give their attention to a story, which must have a definite bearing on the lesson subject. A story can also be used to illustrate a particular point, in the same way that pictures and models are used with the younger children. It can sometimes be a familiar story, in which case the children would be allowed to tell it; this can be very useful as it brings out the value of a well-known story which, from its very familiarity, may have lost some of its meaning.

In a course of lessons on The Beatitudes, the meaning of each one could be made clearer by the telling of a story in which that particular blessedness was shown in terms of a human life. The well-known story of the Good Samaritan could be given a new meaning if linked up with the words, *Blessed are the merciful, for they shall obtain mercy.*

A story can be used at the beginning of a lesson, to arouse the children's interest and set their thoughts in the right direction. If known it would form the Introduction; if new it would come into the first part of the Presentation. A lesson on the Tenth Commandment could very well begin with the story of St Columba and the book that he coveted for, although he did not desire it for himself alone, he went on wanting it after permission to copy it had been refused. Again, a story can be told at the end of the Presentation or, if well known, it could be referred to in the Conclusion, to gather the lesson ideas together and emphasize the main point. A lesson on the meaning of Christmas could end in this way with the story of St Francis and his Crib in the Church at Greccio.

Stories can also be used with a different type of research lesson, when the discoveries are made by *thinking*, instead of by looking up references, etc. For example, in a lesson on Obedience it might be a very good plan to tell two or three stories about people who were obedient to what seemed very strange commands from God, and then let the children think out for themselves how all these stories teach us the value of obedience. Three such stories could be : The Story of the Marriage at Cana of Galilee (John 2. 1-11); the Story of St Joan of Arc; and the Story of Brother Lawrence. The children could talk about the stories and find out for themselves the points of similarity, and draw their own conclusions as to the value of the results of the unquestioning obedience in each case. (Note that the author of the Gospel story points this out in verse 11 : *Jesus . . . manifested forth his glory; and his disciples believed on him.*) Very occasion-ally a lesson can be made up of one continuous story, if it is entirely new and can be divided into episodes. For example, the story of Lord Shaftesbury could be told in this way, and it could be divided up into three episodes : (1) *the Children at Work*, in which his work to get the Factory Acts passed, forbidding the employment of children, would be described; (2) *The Children at School*, in which the story would go on to tell how he used his influence to get schools started for the children who, now that they were released from work, had nothing to do; and (3) *The Children at Home*, in which his work for the clearance of city slums would be described. Even so, the lesson would not be continuous narrative, for a good deal of information could be supplied by the children as to present-day conditions, and these could be contrasted with things as they were in the days of Lord Shaftesbury.

One story can even be spread over two or three con-secutive lessons, each lesson dealing with a definite part of a purpose which applies to all. Three out of a set of lessons on Baptism dealt with the three Baptismal promises : To Renounce, To Believe, and To Obey; and all three were illustrated by a serial story of St Paul. In the first he was shown as renouncing what is wrong when he gave up persecuting the Christians after his conversion; in the second he was shown as believing what is true when he went about preaching to others the things that he believed, and especially when he answered the question of the jailor at Philippi, *Sirs, what must I do to be saved?* with the words : *Believe on the Lord Jesus and thou shalt be saved*; in the third he is shown as obedient to the will of God when he persisted in going to Rome in spite of the many dangers and the opportunity for escape provided by the shipwreck, be-cause he knew that doing what is right is more important than being free. In all these lessons the research method was used so that the children built up the stories for themselves, and at the end they had a useful summary :

> Members of God's Family:
>   Renounce what is wrong,
>   Believe what is true,
>   Do what is right.

A most valuable book of stories to illustrate the religious teaching of children of all ages is *Torches for Teachers*, edited by M. M. Higham.

INDIVIDUAL WORK.   So far we have been considering corporate activities for children in the Junior School. There is also room for individual work to encourage each child to acquire facts and information for himself about the Christian religion. For this purpose two schemes of work have been devised, each of which provides for progressive standards of attainment. They are : *A New Way with Juniors*, C. P. L. Payne; and *Crossbearers*, E. C. Blake, both published by The Church Information Board.

The children are expected to know facts about the Bible, the Prayer Book, the Church Building, and the Christian Year, and to have memorized selected prayers and passages.

CHAPTER 18

METHODS OF TEACHING THE JUNIOR CHILD—II

QUESTIONING. We have noticed that children frequently ask questions; they also love answering them. In any type of lesson we shall find the instruction, "Ask the children if . . .?" or, "Ask them who . . . what . . . how . . . ?" Most people like answering questions because there is something attractive about giving information, and one can be more sure of getting a hearing if the information is given in answer to a question that has been asked. It is also easier to attract the attention of someone else by asking them a question than by merely making a remark, and in the same way it is easier to get the attention of children by asking them a question than by merely offering them information. If they know the answer we can pass on to the next point; if they do not know it, then they will be quite ready to listen to us while we put them in the way of finding it out. We can use questions in order to attract the children's attention at different stages of a lesson. The Introduction can take the form of questioning about a previous lesson to which we wish to link new information, or we can ask questions about some quite familiar thing in everyday life in order to get the right set of ideas into the children's minds. We could introduce a lesson on the Harvest by asking one of the children, "What did you have for breakfast this morning?" At any point during a lesson we may become aware that the attention of the children is wandering, and then a judicious question will recall it and revive interest and attention.

If we are dealing with two or three different aspects of one subject, we can introduce each fresh point with a question and so prevent an awkward break in the lesson. For example, we might be teaching about the Church as (a) the congregation in our own Parish; (b) the Church building in which they worship; and (c) the *Blessed company of all faithful people*. After explaining that the Church in Ephesus would mean the people who made up the congregation, the whole body of Christian people in Ephesus, we could pass to the next aspect by asking the simple questions, "Who should we mean if we spoke of the Church in . . . ?" (naming the place where the children live), and then, "The people in Ephesus had to meet for worship in each other's houses; where does the Church in . . . meet?" Then it can be pointed out that the same word is used for both building and people. Questions can also be asked in the Conclusion stage, either for the purpose of summing up the main points of the lesson, in which case a written summary would be made, or in order that the teacher may make sure that the children have grasped the points of the lesson and, if they have not done so, that errors may be corrected. As we have already seen, a project or research lesson can begin with putting a question to the children and telling them that during the lesson or lessons we hope to be able to find out the answer. At the end of a lesson the children may be given a question on the lesson, to which they will write their own answers.

Sometimes it can be a good plan for the whole of one part of the Presentation stage to be in the form of question and answer, especially if a well-known story is being used to illustrate a point. A lesson on our duty to our neighbour could be illustrated by the story of St Martin, and if well known the children could tell it in answer to questions: "Do you remember how St Martin had a wonderful opportunity of showing himself to be a good neighbour? First of all, who was St Martin?" "Yes, a Bishop, but he was something else before he was a Bishop; what was it?" This would be followed by questions about the life of an officer in the Army in those days, and also on the custom of giving alms by flinging a coin on the ground for beggars to grab. Then would come the questions, "Is this what Martin did to the shivering beggar?" "What *did* he do, then?" "Do you think that was a sensible thing to do?" "What do you suppose his brother officers would have to say about it?" "What would the people in the street say as he rode past in half a cloak?" "What did Martin hear our Lord say about it in his vision?" "Of what words of our Lord in the Gospel does this story remind us?" Then the children would look up Matthew 25. 40, and go on to a study of the parable of the Sheep and the Goats.

In all these different ways of using questions there is the one main purpose, *to make the children think*. This is why it is necessary to have their attention. We have seen that the mental powers of Junior Children are rapidly developing, and we can best help this development by giving them every opportunity of using these powers. They can follow a simple line of reasoning, and asking questions to which we insist on having a thoughtful answer will help them to exercise their reasoning powers, under direction. But the answer must be a thoughtful one and not clever guess work, and in order to ensure this we must observe certain rules when planning our questions. The question asked must be one that cannot be answered by either of the two words, "Yes" or "No", unless immediately followed by one requiring a longer answer. It must generally require a statement of some kind, however simple. On the other hand, it must be a question to which we can reasonably expect the children to be able to give an answer, and not like those once suggested for children of nine on the story of the Good Samaritan, "How many of you have ever helped a wounded man?" "What did you do?" This is in any case a bad type of question, because it is not only unlikely that any of the children will have had an opportunity of helping a wounded man; it is also impossible for a class to answer the question, "How many of you?", in relation to any matter unless it applies to them all, in which case it would not require any thought. The question must be simple, only requiring one answer; we should not say, "Who gave you the message and what did he say?", for this is confusing and would need a very complicated answer. Nor should the question be one to which more than one correct answer could be given, such as, "What did St Paul do?". A question must also be worth answering. Silly questions, such as, "What did he do next?", "Then what did he do?", "What do you think he thought?", etc., will drag a reluctant story from the children and will make them hate it for the rest of their lives; whereas questions which really make them think about the story will give it a new interest, and they will remember the lesson it teaches for all time. Our questions must be quite clear, so that the children know exactly what they are being asked. "It's not very far, is it?" is not clear because the first part makes a statement that it is not very far, and then the second part contradicts it by asking if it is. Also "very far" is too vague, as the "farness" depends so much upon a number of other circumstances. One hundred miles is not very far for a plane, but ten miles is a long way on foot. One more point : questions should vary in difficulty so that both the quick and the slow children may have an equal chance of benefiting from the method, as well as the average children. And the teacher must see that the right child is given the chance of answering the question which suits him best.

It will be seen from what has been said that questioning is an excellent means of procuring the co-operation between teacher and scholars that makes for good relationships, and therefore good order. But for this to be complete there must be opportunity for questions to be asked on both sides. The teacher must be alert to notice signs of a desire to ask a question on the part of any of the children, and to give all the encouragement possible to children who are inclined to be shy.

EXPEDITIONS. However great pains we may take to enable the children to get a good mental picture of the things we describe, and however well we may illustrate our lessons, nothing can ever be quite so helpful as letting them see the real thing with their own eyes. The educational authorities recognized this truth when they began to arrange school journeys for the children in Day Schools; and those engaged in the religious education of children can employ similar methods in a modified form. This applies to other departments as well as to the Junior School, and younger children can, with great advantage, be taken to see some of the things about which they are learning. Such expeditions could be made to their own Parish Church on a weekday, and they could be taken to the country to see the corn growing, or on a visit to a neighbouring farm or market garden. With children over seven we can be more ambitious, and they should be taken to see old Churches, and have such things as rood lofts, wall paintings, aumbries, piscinas, and "squints" explained to them. If at all possible, all children should pay a visit to the Cathedral Church of the Diocese in which they live. Visits could be paid to Picture Galleries, to see some of the great religious masterpieces; to Museums, to see ancient books written by hand and illuminated before the invention of printing, and also some of the results of recent excavations; and to any ruins that may be within reach, especially remains of the Roman occupation of Britain. Children in a class or group should be taken by their own teacher, but two classes might very well join in the same expedition. This will mean giving up some precious hours of free time; but if it is well planned, and not too highly organized, the expedition can be as enjoyable for the teacher as for the children, and there will always be something new to be learnt by all. There can also be nature rambles on summer evenings, and perhaps visits to other residential neighbourhoods, to see how other people live. The children should be encouraged to make suggestions of things they would like to see. These expeditions would be connected in some way with the instruction that was being given in class, which could either precede or follow the visits at the discretion of the teacher. The visits should always be planned with the co-operation of the superintendent of the department.

OTHER METHODS. Many of the methods described for the Kindergarten will still have a place in the teaching of the over-sevens, but their use will be more incidental. The blackboard will be very much in use, but now it will be less for drawing than for writing. Difficult names can be written up for the children to copy; the project, or problem question, should be written out and kept in view throughout the lesson; the question for the written work at the end should also be written out. When a summary is to be worked out, as in the lesson on the Baptismal Promises, each point will be written down as it is made; maps, charts, and diagrams can be drawn and also, occasionally, unfamiliar objects; if the teacher is really an artist he can draw actual pictures, but these should not be attempted by others, as children at this age are very critical. The board can also be very useful for writing up the references to be used during a research lesson.

Pictures are still of great value and can now be smaller, and it is possible to hand them round the class. For this it is a good plan to mount them on a piece of cardboard so that they can stand being handled. The pictures must be good and not too childish. When there are lesson pictures for each child they should be encouraged to mount them in albums.

Models also have their use for new and unfamiliar things, but it is no longer necessary to use them for such well-known things as sheep-folds.

There is still a use for flannelgraph. For example, lessons on Church worship can be illustrated by building up a Church interior, as the lesson proceeds, in much the same way as the building up of a lesson summary.

Junior children will be ready to dramatize a lesson and can now learn parts quite quickly. They can help to plan what shall be done and to choose who shall take the principal parts. But their love of all doing the same thing makes the majority of them quite content to be one of a crowd. These children may not act quite so spontaneously as those in the Kindergarten, but once they are warmed up to it they can do some very fine dramatization, and can also learn to take part in small plays.

CHAPTER 19

CHARACTERISTICS OF CHILDREN
OVER ELEVEN YEARS OF AGE

At, or soon after reaching, the age of eleven years, children in Day School begin to attend one of the various types of Secondary School, and in most parishes a similar change is made in connection with the religious instruction of the children. In some cases the teaching of these children is undertaken by one of the clergy, or some efficient lay person, and the whole of the religious instruction is given by the person in charge. But there are still many parishes where class teaching is given to the children over eleven, and it is necessary for those who are called upon to teach these older children to have a sympathetic understanding of their characteristics.

At about the age of eleven the period of rapid growth and development is often followed by a pause in which the child takes stock of his knowledge and experience, and consolidates his gains, before advancing into the next stage, that of adolescence. Development still goes on, but more steadily, and along more definite lines. One of the most important characteristics at this time is a growing *spirit of independence*, as a result of which the child becomes impatient of control. The child of eleven or twelve does not like to be asked where he is going—often he does not know; but he is willing enough on his return to say where he has been, if the information is asked as a matter of interest and not demanded as a right. At this age a boy or a girl will sometimes take long, solitary walks or cycle rides, and during these excursions much hard thinking is often done, and conclusions are reached and stored up until wider experience of life will cause them to be reconsidered. For the time being opinions so formed will be tenaciously held and it is, therefore, important that the child should be supplied with sufficient and suitable material for thought, while being allowed to think things out for himself. He should be encouraged to consider various different points of view, so that he may develop sound judgement and a good sense of proportion. Independence of thought and of action will develop side by side and each is necessary to the other, for thought prompts action and action stimulates thought; an unreasonable check upon either will hinder both. A child who is never allowed to be alone may never learn to face up to, and attempt to resolve, the problems in his life. At this age a child seems to have very little conscious need of the adult—except as the provider of material needs, which he takes for granted—and he is no longer prepared to accept information or admonition without question. He will still ask for opinions, and sometimes even for advice, but the answer given will be regarded as only one among many possible solutions of his problem, and he will decide for himself whether to accept or reject what he is told. So we must not expect him always to agree with us, but must be ready to see, and discuss with him, other points of view than our own; nor must we expect him to be willing to do with us the things that we want to do, though we should welcome any desire on his part for us to do with him the things that he likes to do. Such occasions may be rare, but he is genuinely pleased if we can really share his interests.

All this may seem to suggest that the child over eleven is to be allowed to do exactly as he pleases, from now onwards, without regard for anyone else; but this is not really intended. If the child has been trained in a right understanding of Christian principles and conduct he will already be, at least to some extent, a disciplined person. He is nearing what the Prayer Book describes as *years of discretion*, defined by the Concise Oxford Dictionary as the time at which one is fit to manage oneself. The meaning of the word *discretion* is given as liberty of deciding as one thinks fit, absolutely or within limits. In the case of the eleven year old it is only *within limits* that he should be allowed this liberty. Many of these limits will be of the child's own choosing or devising. A schoolboy or schoolgirl would not dream of doing the thing that *is not done*. At one time it will be correct to carry books in a satchel, but a little later the satchel must be discarded and the books carried in some other way—prescribed by school tradition, not by the school authorities. Habits that have been acquired in earlier childhood will also exercise a definite control. A child who has once formed the habit of tidying up after a picnic in the country, will not be likely to leave litter about when left to himself. Other limitations are imposed by the society in which he lives: the law of the land, the rules of the school, the family standard of good manners; these cannot be broken with impunity. But these are all forms of external pressure, and it is of vital importance to the child's later adult life that he should learn the meaning and value of control from within.

It is precisely at this stage that the Prayer Book recommends that the child shall be brought to the Bishop to receive the gift of the Holy Spirit in Confirmation. For what purpose? Surely it is that he may be guided, strengthened, and inspired by the Holy Spirit to fulfil the Baptismal promises which he renews: to renounce, to believe, and to obey. This means that the time is now coming for the gradual transference of the child from external, human control to the inner control of the Holy Spirit. For this receiving of the Holy Spirit in Confirmation, preparation is necessary, and one of the most important parts of such preparation is a sense of need on the part of the child. How can he realize his own inadequacy, if he is so constantly shepherded by those who are anxious for his welfare that he has no chance to develop a sense of need? Life presents us all with a succession of opportunities for making choices, of greater or lesser importance. In time, many of the daily choices become habitual and are, therefore, made without conscious effort. Habits so formed may be good or bad, and character is, to a large extent, determined by the kind of choices which have become habitual. For example, the person who can be relied upon to be punctual is one who has consistently chosen to be so until he has become a punctual person. In a similar way spiritual development is largely a matter of making choices—learning at each stage, with God's help, *To refuse the evil and choose the good*; and God, in His wisdom, has endowed us with freewill so that our choice may be willing and not enforced. It is thus reasonable to conclude that the desire to exercise this freedom of choice is as God-given as the gift itself, and that its use is necessary to our spiritual growth. We must, therefore, be prepared *to stand back* and give the child who is showing a desire for independence increasing opportunities for making his own choices; as well as *to stand by* to render help in case of need. The advice once given to parents, "Let your children live dangerously," can well be applied to their spiritual training. The more we can assure the child of eleven to thirteen that we are willing to leave him alone, so far as his leisure and recreations are concerned, the more ready will he be to come to us when in real need. This will give us the opportunity of telling him—in a simple matter-of-fact way—of the work of the Holy Spirit in the Church, and in the lives of individual men and women.

Unfortunately, many children reach *years of discretion* without having had the advantage of Christian training, and with them the natural impatience of control leads to unruly, and often destructive, behaviour. When this is the case it is extremely doubtful whether the inexperienced class teacher

7

can help them, for they need expert handling. So far as organized religious education is concerned, this difficulty should not often arise, for children in this age-group will normally have been through the other departments and, if the teaching given in these has been satisfactory, they should be ready to respond to the new methods suited to their age. Such unruliness as occurs with these children is generally due to an unsatisfied desire for independence, and the remedy is not repression, but greater freedom. If a child at this age is unduly thwarted, or coerced, he may develop an anti-social attitude which will lead to delinquency; but if he is allowed to *feel* free, the desire to rebel will disappear. A child of this age, who had spent an afternoon rowing about on the river in a dinghy with a grown-up companion, suddenly said, "I do love being with you because I can do what I like". The grown-up might truthfully have responded, "I do love being with you because you are no trouble"!

From what has been said it will be seen that boys and girls at this age are individuals who must be treated as such, and not merely regarded as "the children". One way of doing this is by encouraging the *sense of responsibility* which is now beginning to develop. This is not very easily recognized, and in many ways the child will appear to be entirely irresponsible. This is because he no longer enjoys doing things merely for the sake of doing them, and loses interest if they do not seem to be worth doing for their own sake. He is definitely bored if, in addition to being told what to do, he is told exactly how to do it, for a great part of his enjoyment will be in finding out *how* to do it for himself. If he—or she—is given responsibility, and realizes that the success of an enterprise depends upon his doing his part well, he will rise to the occasion and show himself to be thoroughly trustworthy. Should he elect to cycle on an expedition where others are walking, and be given the food to carry, or commissioned to have a fire lit and the kettle boiling before the others arrive, he can be counted upon to carry out his part. The success of a play can be assured if each member of the cast be made responsible for the properties necessary for his or her part. Most boys and girls of this age can be entrusted with the temporary charge of a younger child. They do not usually seek responsibility, as they are only beginning to realize that they can carry it; but they like to feel that they are being trusted, and while not being overburdened they should be increasingly treated as responsible persons. A girl who was reproached for behaving in a childish way complained that she was treated as a child. The reply was that when she behaved as an older child she should be treated as such; but she argued that it was the other way round; if only they would treat her as a responsible being, it would help her to live up to it. The child was right, she needed responsibility to help her to grow to her full stature of girlhood.

The child over eleven can safely be trusted, if the right appeal is made, because he is beginning to set himself very *high standards*, and he is genuinely distressed when he fails to live up to them. Sometimes these can be a little embarrassing to older people who do not understand their purpose, as in the case of a small group of schoolgirls aged twelve and thirteen who agreed to break, systematically, what they considered to be tiresome and unnecessary little school regulations, and made it a point of honour that when warned of the approach of authority they should go on doing the forbidden thing, be caught in the act, pay the penalty, and do it again. If one of them should be caught alone and sent to the Headmistress, the others were to go with her and share the blame. The code of honour is not usually as extreme as this; but it may often be that what seems very singular behaviour is inspired by a high, even if mistaken, ideal.

In more normal ways boys and girls set themselves high standards of accomplishment in schoolwork, handicrafts,

and games, and they often suffer from an acute dissatis-
faction with their own work. A handwork teacher is often
exasperated by the way a child will suddenly destroy a
nearly completed piece of work, because it was not good
enough. One child who was musical gave up learning to play
both piano and violin, because she could not bear to hear
her own faulty playing. Essays will be written and re-
written, and in the end a very barren piece of work offered,
because the child feels unable to give satisfactory expression
to what he really wants to say. Children may need a lot of
help through this period of self-discouragement, which they
should be led to recognize as evidence of their need of
spiritual strength.

—In human relationships their sense of loyalty to an ideal is
very strong, especially with regard to promises. These older
children are often reluctant to make a promise because they
realize its binding nature, but once a promise is given it will
certainly be kept.

This loyalty to a high standard, if rightly directed, can be
a means of training these children in loyalty to the vow they
are soon to make for themselves in Confirmation. If the
Christian ideal can be presented to them as something
tremendously worth while, and if they are encouraged to
think out for themselves *how* they can plan to live up to it
by the grace of the Holy Spirit, then the solemnity of the
simple *I do* will be more fully realized and it will become a
point of honour to keep it.

These high standards are helping the child to develop a
critical faculty which will be brought to bear on other people
and things, as well as upon himself. He will contrast and
compare, and condemn outright anything that falls below
his own standard of what is correct. Especially will he be
critical in matters of religion, and here he will be tremendously helped if he is allowed to investigate for himself the
grounds of our Christian Faith. While not attempting to

hide, or explain away, the Church's failures of which he is critical, we can enable him to discover, through a study of Church History, the miracle of the Church's survival through the manifold perils that have threatened her very life again and again; and can also help him to see that in every age, not least in our own, the Church is made up of individual men and women with human frailties, and that she can only become a perfect instrument in the hands of God when each individual member is allowing the Holy Spirit to rule in his or her heart.

Along with this critical faculty there is a strong *sense of the ridiculous* which can at times be very disconcerting. Much of the failure, in the past, of attempts to give adequate religious instruction to these children, has been due to the use of undignified or unworthy methods which fell below the standards set by Day School, and consequently merited their scorn. The simple coloured pictures suitable for young children are quite out of place and will only provoke mirth, and some of the best-loved children's hymns will seem ridiculous to the older children. In one parish where Sunday School was held at the same time as a service in Church, the choir boys were never able to attend the School. On one occasion, however, they were sent to take part in an open session at which all the departments were present. Hymns had been chosen to meet all needs, and the older scholars understood this perfectly well and were able to join with the Nursery children in singing, *Praise Him, praise Him, all ye little children*, which the little ones in front sang with their usual actions. But to the choir boys it was merely funny, and their behaviour would have ruined the whole session had the small children not been too intent on what they were doing to notice.

These older children must be introduced to all that is best in art, literature, and music. Copies of Old Masters can be obtained in picture postcard size, and they are of very great value for our purpose, for these medieval painters so often set their great, central figures against an exquisite miniature background of busy daily life in which can be seen farmers at work in their fields, merchants travelling to and fro, ships being laden or unladen, all showing the artist's consciousness of the close relationship between religion and life. In these pictures there are often little touches which arouse joyous amusement, but nothing to call forth ridicule, and so they will help to educate the children's sense of humour. There is often much humour to be found in the sculptured decorations of ancient Cathedrals and Churches as, for example, the Imp in Lincoln Cathedral, and the less well-known place in the same Cathedral where the sculptor, engaged in the decoration of a series of pillars with foliage, seems suddenly to have been seized with a spirit of mischief for we find, peeping out at us from amongst the leaves, a cat catching a mouse. This impulse shows how close, to this unknown sculptor, religion was to life. Children would enjoy visiting some of these ancient Churches and being allowed to hunt for touches of humour, and it would help them to realize that religion is a joyous thing.

Because of their high standards, boys and girls show a very great *sensitiveness*, especially to criticism or ridicule, the two things in which they themselves excel. This is to be expected, since either criticism or ridicule will suggest that they have failed in their ideal; and for this reason, too, they are quick to be on the defensive. At this time it is more than ever important that we should not play on their feelings, for the sense of failure can become almost unbearable and we must not add to it the misery of having hurt someone they love. Although they like to tease others, they are not very ready to be teased, unless it is by someone they are quite sure they can trust. Such teasing must be as man to man, not by someone taking an unfair advantage of a superior position. A teacher should never tease a boy or a girl in class.

This suggests another characteristic of children at this age : their keen *sense of justice*. One of their most frequent condemnations is, "It's not fair". They are utterly scornful of anyone who does not play fair at games, and any sign of favouritism wins their instant disapproval. Some children who had not got on well with a previous teacher confided to her successor, "She had favourites, you know". But their sense of justice cuts both ways, and they are scrupulously fair even when it goes against themselves. One of two schoolboys had been charged with a fault of which the other was guilty, and had been told to report to the Headmaster in the afternoon. The real culprit was asked, "Surely you are not going to let John be caned for something you have done?", but they explained that it was quite all right, "because Tom has often been licked for things he hasn't done". No doubt, also, John had often escaped a caning for things he *had* done, so it was all fair on balance !

All these characteristics of the older child can only be discovered by long and patient experience, for he does not readily give himself away. One of the most noticeable things about him is his *reserve*, which is probably his means of self-protection in a world that he has begun to find can be hostile. Any attempts to question him about his thoughts or feelings will make him close up like a sea anemone in a rock pool, which closes when touched. He can live in a family circle and remain entirely aloof from it, and the other members may have no idea as to what is going on in his mind, nor whether he has any interest in them at all. This reserve should be respected, for it is a sign that he is realizing himself as a person, and it is as persons that we are called, individually, to the service of God. If we try to force his confidence he may become sullen, and we shall also run the risk of turning his thoughts in upon himself instead of leaving him free to direct them outwardly upon the world around him, of which he is becoming so intensely aware.

The child at this age has his own natural safeguard against becoming too interested in himself for, although he does like to spend a fair amount of his time alone, he is at the same time developing a *spirit of co-operation*. This enables him to do things with others, preferably of his own age, and he is now able to make his own personal contribution to what is being done. Boys and girls at this age no longer all like to do the same thing, but in any enterprise each will have his or her allotted part. They have many mysterious undertakings from which the unsympathetic grown-up is excluded, but should one come across them unawares one would see them all doing different things which are part of a whole plan. A simple illustration of this can be seen at the seaside. Young children will all be digging holes or trenches in the sand, or making sand pies. When a little older, they attempt to build castles; but although two or three may be at work on the same building, they will all be doing the same kind of thing to it. But the children over eleven will embark upon an elaborate fortification, or railway system, and each of the workers will concentrate on a different part, although they will all be working to a common plan. So it is with their more usual occupations, and it is often difficult to discover if any one of them is recognized as a leader. Usually these children go about in quite small groups of five or six at the most, and although the groups dissolve from time to time, and re-form, for considerable periods of time the same children will always be seen together. Parents often see very little of these older children during holiday times, for when not out alone they are sure to be "out with the boys", or "with the girls".

Sometimes within these groups we can see the beginnings of very real friendship between two boys, or two girls, and these can be of immense value to both, for the stronger one is really moulding the other and, at the same time, developing his own powers of leadership. The wise parent or teacher will watch such friendships carefully, and be ready to help when necessary, because there is a danger that the two friends may become self-absorbed and anti-social to the rest of the family or group, and also a possibility of the one dominating the other and so preventing his free development. Where the right relationship exists the friends will do things together with the same spirit of co-operation as the group.

Because of this ability to co-operate these children now take a keen interest in highly organized games such as cricket, football, netball, hockey, or lacrosse, and can forget their own triumphs in their eagerness for the success of their side. They also enjoy team games and relay races, and any form of activity in which they can play for their side. This spirit of co-operation plays a very important part in their training for full membership in the Church, and will enable them to understand the meaning of St Paul's words, *Now there are diversities of gifts, but the same Spirit* (1 Corinthians 12. 4).

CHAPTER 20

WERE it not for this spirit of co-operation, we might be tempted to feel that we were contemplating an impossible task when we talk of teaching children over eleven. The Secondary Schools have facilities which are quite beyond the reach of the class teacher in voluntary religious education, and it is unwise to attempt to compete with them since our failure will inevitably provoke scornful comparisons. Fortunately, this is not necessary: it was said in an earlier chapter that the meaning of *teaching* is a sharing of something that we have with someone who has less than we have, or none at all; and again, that the true function of teaching is to make available for the next generation knowledge that has been gained in the past. This will remind us that we have not to try to pump information into these reserved and critical children, but to provide them with the opportunity of discovering the information for themselves, and to offer them such help in the discovery as we are able to give through knowing a little more about it than they do at present. Often we shall find that on certain points they know more about it than we do, and then the work will be real co-operation, for we shall be able to pool our information and all learn from each other.

THE PROJECT METHOD. This understanding of our task will help us to realize the value of the project method, which can be used much more freely with these older children than with the Juniors. The true project is one in which the children themselves take the initiative, though the teacher will probably find that he has to provoke the questions which can be used as the basis for a project.

In a Day School this method can be very much elaborated, and the project can be extended to other subjects than the one out of which it arises. For example, questions asked by the children in a lesson on the Lord's Prayer might lead to a discussion in the geography period on means of transport at the time of St Augustine; in the history period on conditions of life in England at that time; in the literature period on different languages and the difficulties of translation. These in turn might suggest other topics which would widen the field of inquiry, and lead the children far beyond the original subject of the Lord's Prayer. Questions asked in the history lesson might arouse interest in Canterbury Cathedral, and so lead to a study of mediæval architecture in the art class; and of Dorothy L. Sayers' play, *The Zeal of Thine House*, in the literature period!

It is obvious that such a method could not be followed in a class which only meets for a short period once a week, but where there is a weekday activity in the hands of the same leaders as the organization in which religious instruction is given, and where there are really competent teachers, individual classes can follow out the method. The important point is that the initiative as to any particular subject for investigation must come from the *class*, even though the work done is very different from that which the teacher had in mind at the outset. The experienced teacher will watch for the question arising in any one lesson which will suggest a fresh piece of group work.

A teacher may have roughed out a scheme for studying the Christian Ministry, and have reached the point at which St Augustine landed in Kent, when a question from one of the children might arouse interest in the monastic system. This would offer great opportunities for study, for the monasteries at their best were the seats of learning for students and professors; the houses where priests were trained; the centres of culture—it was here that many early theological works were written, and ancient writings copied, the work all being done by hand and wonderfully illuminated; and here, too, all that was best in architecture, painting, sculpture, and such handicrafts as weaving and dyeing, were employed in the building and decorating of the monastic buildings and the Abbey Churches. The monasteries were also the places where children were taught, the naked clothed, the hungry fed, and the sick tended; and the monks were occupied in husbandry, carpentry, and many homely crafts. This would provide a syllabus for many weeks, but more probably the class would select one or two of these subjects only, and from these others would develop. It would be for the teacher to hold the reins, and see that the interest did not wander too far afield and become wholly unrelated to the main purpose of the project.

In connection with these subjects there could be many varied activities. Children who could draw would like to make their own sketches of architectural features in the neighbourhood; others might prefer to practise lettering; there might be a few who would like to study the history, and write out accounts, of the different great monastic foundations; there could be a collection of postcard pictures from Old Masters; and musical children could be interested in Church music. Some of the handicrafts could be learnt at the weekday organization.

This is an ambitious programme which would be beyond the bounds of possibility for ordinary class teaching alone, and the teacher may have to be content to adapt and modify some of the lesser characteristic methods of the true project.

In one parish a small class of girls aged eleven and twelve seemed quite unable to settle to any constructive work. At last the leader said, "What would you really *like* to do?"

Almost at once they said they would like "to do the miracles". After some discussion it was decided that, after studying them carefully, they should write out all the miracles of our Lord in everyday language—each girl taking a different miracle week by week—and then make them all up into a Book of Miracles. The leader undertook to provide the necessary materials, and procured a loose-leaf file into which the miracles could be fitted in order. The children set themselves a very high standard in both English and neatness, and the pages were beautifully written. They worked together on the same task, yet each had her own piece of work to do, and the teacher was there to give them any help for which they might ask. When completed, the work was to be followed by the more difficult task of studying and then writing out the parables of our Lord in the same way.

A class of choir boys arranged that they should take it in turn to select a subject for discussion, and that each one should introduce his own subject to the class. As it was a Bible Class there was a stipulation that it must be a Bible subject.

It is not possible to suggest very definite projects for the use of teachers because of the importance of their being initiated by the children, but questions asked by children could lead to a study of such social and industrial problems as bad housing, road accidents, strikes, etc. In connection with such study a Christian Newspaper might be produced. Or the children might embark upon a study of outstanding persons in the Old Testament and this could prompt the writing and production—including the making of scenery and properties—of a Biblical play or pageant. The teacher who is going to use this method must be full of resource, and as ready to co-operate as he wishes his scholars to be.

THE RESEARCH METHOD. As with the project, it is possible to make much fuller use of the research method with Secondary children than with Juniors, and in almost any type of lesson there will be a place for reseach. The teacher of these older children should be prepared to provide them with any books they will be likely to need, and it is a good plan to collect a small library of suitable ones, or to make a note of books that could be borrowed on occasions from friends. The children should have their own Bibles, Prayer Books, and Hymn Books, but they will often need such other books as dictionaries, history books, books of poems, and atlases. If there is a weekday activity there should be a lending library from which members can borrow books on the lives of Saints, and biographies of great men and women who have served their fellow men. The children should also be encouraged to join the children's section of the Public Library and to carry out some of their researches there. The teacher should possess or have access to a good commentary, and this should, when necessary, be available for the use of the children.

Owing to lack of space and equipment, research work in class may, in some cases, have to be confined to the Bible and Prayer Book. A course of lessons on the Eucharist could be taken with the help of these alone. In one or two lessons the connection between the Christian Offering and the sacrificial system of the Jews could be traced. The teacher would open the discussion by telling the children something of the inner meaning of the sacrifices offered by the Jews, and the human need to which they gave expression. The children would then be encouraged to find and read in the Old Testament the various regulations for the offering of sacrifices, and the different kinds that were offered. They would also look at the many denunciations by the prophets against sacrifices that had lost their inner meaning and were mere outward show, having no moral or spiritual significance at all. Having written down brief notes of the information collected and pooled, they would then turn to Hebrews, and see how a very early Christian taught that all that had been foreshadowed in these early sacrifices had been perfectly fulfilled in Christ. Finally, reference to the Communion Service in the Prayer Book would enable them to relate all that they had discovered to the Eucharist. They would see that we can make this Offering our own by pleading before God that perfect Sacrifice, and offering ourselves in union with the Offering of our Lord, *souls and bodies, to be a reasonable, holy and living sacrifice unto Thee.* A final talk from the teacher would gather all these points together, and during each week the children would write up their notes.

This is the simplest form of research work. With other subjects each child would be given a different piece of research to do, as far as possible according to his particular bent, and the work begun in class would be continued throughout the week. All would deal with different aspects of the same subject—for instance, the work of the Church in Central Africa. One child would undertake to study the geography and to produce maps; another would read up and write a brief life of David Livingstone; a third would undertake to study some of the literature of the Universities' Mission to Central Africa, and write out a brief account of its history; others would study questions of climate, means of transport, native administration, evils introduced by the white man, native customs, and any other relevant subjects. At the next and following classes the children would each make their own contribution and help to build up a comprehensive picture of the work of the Church in Central Africa.

THE DISCUSSION METHOD. When reading lesson notes one frequently comes across the words, "Discuss this", and with the older children practically every type of lesson will include discussion, just as they will nearly all include some form of research. Generally these discussions will be quite informal and spontaneous, arising out of some question that has been asked, or some statement that has been questioned. But on occasions the class could very well become a real discussion group. In a school, this might be part of a plan which included the whole department, when the superintendent would give an introductory talk and then each class would be given one or more questions to discuss. But it is also possible for a class teacher to plan a discussion lesson, probably as the result of a point having been raised, at a previous class, which was too extensive to be dealt with at the time. He would then say that a whole lesson period should be given up to it later on. When the time has been arranged, the child who raised the point could be asked to make a brief statement of his point of view, and if he had been opposed, the opposer would be given a similar opportunity. Then the matter would be open to discussion, speakers being limited to time, and no one allowed to speak a second time so long as there were others who wanted to speak. It would probably be best for the teacher to act as chairman until the children were used to the method, when different children would be voted into the chair.

In the case of the research lessons described above, on the Church in Central Africa, each child would open the discussion on his particular subject by reading his paper. He or she would then invite questions, and so the discussion would start. In order to take part in it the children would have been encouraged not to confine their researches to their own subject but, while concentrating on that, to do some all-round reading as well. At the end of the discussion the chairman would sum up, and the class write up the summary.

FILMSTRIPS. These are a useful form of illustration, particularly for the older boys and girls. They can also prove a valuable means of provoking discussion. There are many useful strips on the background of the Bible, on the Church Services, and on the lives of great Christians. The S.P.C.K. Filmstrip Guide gives full information about strips, their cost, their hire, and hire charges for projectors.

All these methods may appear to be rather ambitious, and it will usually take a little time and much patience before the children are able to let themselves go, and enter into the spirit of the schemes; but once they have got into their stride they will appreciate the fact that they are being treated as reasonable beings, and co-operate happily in their work.

CHAPTER 21

THE CATECHISM METHOD. The true catechism method is one of many alternative forms of organization for the religious instruction of children and, as such, has properly no place here. But the principles underlying the method can be applied to class teaching. The method is not new, but was first used in France in the year 1870 by Mgr. Dupanloup, a spiritual genius with a great love of children who, for this reason, was able to apply the method with a success which others less gifted might not be able to achieve. It was based on a belief that something which had once been memorized became a permanent possession, and it was, therefore, a vital necessity for the children to possess in this way the great doctrinal truths of the Christian Faith. Put more bluntly the idea was rather like this : children can learn very easily by heart, and will be less able to do so later on; so we will encourage them to memorize everything that it is necessary for them to know while they can learn it, and then as time goes on they will come to understand what it means. This view is no longer generally held, as it is felt by most teachers that children should understand what they learn. But for a very different reason some teachers still use the method in a modified form. There is a school of thought which considers that the pause in development already referred to, which occurs round about the age of eleven, is a sign of exhaustion after the previous rapid growth, and that the child needs a rest period. For this reason we should not require too much mental effort from these children, but should concentrate on their ability to learn by heart, and trust that what they learn in this way will become filled with fuller meaning later on. In its simplest form the teacher writes on a blackboard (a large one would be required) a series of questions with their answers for the children to see. He then gives an instruction on the subject matter with which the questions deal, to show how the answers were worked out. The children might discuss this a little, and ask questions, after which they copy out the questions and answers and learn them by heart. The following week they are asked the questions and are required to answer them from memory. This is in keeping with the method of the Church Catechism in the Prayer Book, and with the rubric at the end requiring that the Curate of every Parish shall *openly in the Church instruct and examine . . . children . . . in some part of this Catechism*; and is an application of its principles to other subjects. The method, however, does not entirely meet the needs of children of Secondary School age.

SELF-TEACHING.   This is in complete contrast to the method of the catechism, for here all the work in class is done by the children themselves. The scheme of study is planned by the teacher beforehand, and certain tasks set for the children to carry out with the help of books of reference. It is a form of research work, but is individual instead of corporate, and appeals to that side of the child that likes to go off alone and think things out for himself. It should not be used continuously, but could be carried out over a short period of five or six weeks, at infrequent intervals. Usually the children are all given the same task, but this method could be combined with a corporate activity in which each was working on one aspect of a larger subject with a view to pooling information at the end of the period. The method is useful when a class is either too large, or in a room with too many other classes, for it to be possible to have questions and discussions; or in country schools where one teacher has to have a few children of all ages in one class. In this last case the older children can be doing individual work while the teacher is taking a lesson with the younger ones. When the class has the undivided attention of the teacher, it is a good plan for each piece of work to be submitted to him as it is completed, before the next piece is commenced, so that any mistakes may be corrected while the work is fresh in the child's mind. The teacher should also be ready to answer any questions about the work the child may want to ask. Should he find that all the children are puzzled over the same point he may stop the work and give a brief instruction on that point to them all together. When all the children are doing the same work a spirit of competition can be introduced.

The work might be planned out like this : if the subject to be studied were The Life and Work of St Paul, the title would be written across the top of the work-paper or card. Underneath, the questions would be written on the left-hand side of the page, and the references on the right. Each child would have an exercise book in which to write the answers.

THE LIFE AND WORK OF ST PAUL

1. What do we know about St Paul before he became a Christian?   Acts 13. 9; 22. 3; Philippians 3. 4-6; Acts 21. 37; 22. 25-28.

2. Trace a map of the Mediterranean and mark in Tarsus and Jerusalem.   See Atlas.

3. Write out the story of St Paul's Conversion.   Acts 9. 1-19; 22. 3-21; 26. 9-19.

The rest of the work-paper would be on similar lines, introducing as much variety as possible. Quicker children might eventually get a whole lesson period ahead of the others, and for them additional work would have to be prepared, or they might be kept level with the others by being allowed to read a book about St Paul when the work set for each week was completed.

THE COMPANIONSHIP METHOD. This method incorporates the best features of both the catechism method and self-teaching, by providing a scheme of individual work for the children within the framework of group instruction and worship. In its fully developed form it embraces all the activities of the organization in which the older children receive their religious instruction, and is thus the responsibility of the leader or superintendent. But the method is extremely flexible, and can readily be adapted for class teaching.

The individual work is an interesting and progressive scheme planned in a series of Tests : Novice Tests, Pilgrim Tests, and Companion Tests, with a selection of optional Further Tests. Each Test has six sections, with work related to Prayer, Bible, Catechism, the story of the Christian Church, personal service, and Church buildings. When the set work has been satisfactorily completed a badge is awarded for each section of the Test. These are already gummed and can be affixed at once to the Test Card in the space provided.

Full details of the method can be found in *The Companionship Method*, T. A. Rockley, published by The Church Information Board.

DRAMATIZATION. We are concerned only with group or class teaching, but reference has already been made to the writing and production of plays, and there are also less ambitious ways in which older children can be encouraged to dramatize. It has sometimes been said that children over eleven cannot act because they are too self-conscious, but it has been proved that this is not the case if they are properly prepared. The mistake that is so often made is to use them as stage properties and to try to make them do what *we* should do if we were taking the part, instead of letting them interpret the part according to their own natural genius. It is constant rehearsing and the hammering-in of instructions that make the children self-conscious, not the impersonation of a character. Children over eleven can act extremely well, and put into acting something which is peculiarly their own. A small boy of eleven, who was to be one of the Kings in a Christmas Play, was taken to see a play by expert amateurs the week before his own performance. The children's play took place in the Parish Church and, when the time came, that small boy walked up the Church with an unconscious dignity which surpassed that of the adult performer, whose actor's trick of walking slowly with apparently long strides he had caught perfectly. The boy was a King, every inch of him—but not the same kind of King as the man !

Perhaps the most suitable form of dramatizing for children of this age is miming, when the part is played without speech either during or following the reading of the words by a narrator. With this method the acting can be almost spontaneous, and in any case should not be more than once rehearsed. This has been tried with considerable success. Opportunities for such acting can often be found in a parish : a class could undertake to dramatize a Bible or missionary story for the Kindergarten; the children could act a play as part of an entertainment for parents, or a Mothers' Union gathering; one group of children presented a missionary play at a Sunday School Festival.

A very successful attempt at miming was carried out by some children of eleven to fourteen on Christmas Day. A combined service had been arranged for children of all ages, including a Nursery School, and these older children were asked if they would help by acting the Christmas story, so that the little ones could *see* it, as well as hear it. They agreed, and met on Christmas Eve to arrange what should be done. Fortunately, the parish possessed a good supply of home-made eastern garments and other properties, and the children were easily fitted out with clothing. The service was to be held in a large hall with a platform and curtain, and the plan was for the narrator to tell the story in very simple language especially suited to the little ones, and for the mimers to fit their actions to the telling of the story. They then went on to plan what they would each do, but not *how* they were going to do it, which was left for each one to work out for him- or herself; the idea in the mind of the producer being that they should interpret the characters in their own way. To this end she suggested to the children the kind of thoughts which would be in the minds of the people they were representing, so that they might get the *feel* of the part each one was to play. The final plan was that the platform should be the Stable, and a low seat was prepared for MARY: that, and the Manger, were all the furnishings necessary. The ANGELS were to be concealed behind the door at one side of the stage, and the SHEPHERDS on the other side, at the top of the stairs leading from the hall to the stage. Near the foot of these stairs was a swing door, and this was to be the Inn, the INNKEEPER and his BOY being in readiness on the other side. MARY and JOSEPH and the THREE KINGS were to wait in a room at the far end of the Hall.

On Christmas morning the children came and, when dressed, took up their appointed places, and the service began. As the story of the journey to Bethlehem was told, MARY and JOSEPH came up the Hall and knocked at the Inn door, only to learn that there was no room. As they turned away the BOY ran after them and brought them back, and they were shown the Stable. As MARY sank on to the seat the curtain was pulled (by the INNKEEPER).

While the congregation were singing *While Shepherds watched their flocks by night*, the SHEPHERDS crept in and took up their place below the platform. The story then proceeded, and the children, left entirely to themselves, rose to the occasion and did all that was required with complete composure. When the narrator spoke of the bright light, the curtain parted and the ANGEL GABRIEL appeared, to be followed at the right moment by two smaller ANGELS, one on each side, who all three together said the *Gloria in Excelsis Deo*. Then followed the singing of *O little town of Bethlehem*, while the SHEPHERDS set out to find the Stable; and then the curtain was drawn to show the Manger Scene, which had been arranged entirely by the children themselves. The only help had been suggestions that JOSEPH should guard MARY, the two smaller ANGELS the Manger, and GABRIEL should be the guardian of the whole scene. These ideas had been beautifully expressed, and the little ANGELS, one at each end of the Manger, were completely absorbed in their task, while the Nursery children were almost too rapt to join in the singing of their own special hymn, *Away in a Manger*. The story then went on to the worship of the SHEPHERDS, and the offerings of the KINGS, who came up, one by one, from the back of the Hall while the narrator sang the three solo verses of *We three Kings of Orient are*. Finally, the whole congregation of children made an act of worship, singing *O come, all ye faithful*.

The chief note of the whole thing was its simplicity, and this was helped by the complete naturalness of the children who took part. Had they been rehearsed and drilled, this would have been lost entirely, and as the play in itself was too simple to be otherwise effective it might have been a complete failure. As it was, the children repeated it for their parents and friends on the following Sunday, when Bible readings were substituted for the telling of the story, and in spite of the greater strain neither the simplicity nor the naturalness was lost.

Dramatization is only of real value to the children themselves if it is a true expression by them of something from within. This value is enhanced if, at the same time, they can feel that they are handing on to others something which they know to be worth while. On the occasion described above the children were both offering a personal act of devotion, and also handing on the Christmas message to the children younger than themselves. But it is not always essential to have an audience, and children who have a room of their own can very usefully write, and enact on the spot, short dramatizations of any particular episode they may have been studying. Episodes in Church History could be deeply impressed on their minds in this way, and this would enable them to realize the wonder of the Church's inextinguishable vitality. At the end of such a series the episodes might be put together to form the basis of something in the nature of a Pageant, to be performed more publicly when an occasion should offer.

OTHER METHODS. The Story will still have a place, as it has in all instruction, and it can be used in many different ways. The teacher should always be on the look-out for short stories that can be stored up in the mind and produced when opportunity arises. In the course of discussion a difficult point may often be cleared up by the telling of a story that just fits, or by reference to one that is very well known. Some people have a gift for making up a story, in the nature of a parable or an allegory, on the spot, and these can often clear up a difficulty. Sometimes a child may like to tell a story that seems to bear on the subject under discussion, or the children might try their hand at making up a story, individually or corporately, to illustrate something they have discovered to be important. Children could at other times be given a story to read, either in class or during the week, and this would form the basis of discussion.

Expeditions are still of great value, and can be more definitely educational. Sketches can be made or photographs taken, comparisons made, and records kept.

Handwork also has its place, though now it would more definitely be a craft. Where there is accommodation available in a parish there should be something in the nature of a workshop, where there is a carpenter's bench and necessary tools, a small loom, a sewing machine, and materials for the various crafts. A Parochial Church Council might find such a workshop very useful for running repairs to Church fittings and Hall furnishings. Children could do basket weaving and leather work in their weekday organization. Some of the children might learn to braille, and they could undertake a regular correspondence with blind children; they might all usefully learn the manual deaf and dumb alphabet, which may at any time prove unexpectedly helpful. A diner at a restaurant realized that her opposite neighbour was in difficulties with the waitress and, guessing the reason, questioned her with her hands, and was able to put matters right. Although deaf children are now taught to lip-read, there are still many older deaf people who can only speak with their hands, and have not learned to lip-read. There is also a large number of people who are both deaf and blind, and for them the manual language is the only means of communication.

The following books would be helpful to those who are responsible for the religious instruction of children over eleven years of age : *Teaching Doctrine*, by Phyllis Dent; *The Confirmation School*, *The Teaching of the Church Catechism* and *The Teaching of the Book of Common Prayer*, all three by A. R. Browne-Wilkinson; *Teaching Religious Knowledge*, by B. R. Youngman (University of London Press).

CHAPTER 22

CONCLUSION

In a short study such as this it is only possible to generalize, and there is a risk of appearing to suggest that all children of a given age are alike. This is, of course, not the case, since no two persons are ever exactly alike. In children there are individual differences of every kind, physical and mental, and in any group there will always be quick and slow, lively and quiet, attractive and unresponsive children, so that when we speak of the more average child we are merely referring to the child who comes somewhere between these various extremes. Besides these individual differences there are also group differences. Children in the north share the northern characteristics, just as children in the south share southern characteristics; children who live in the country differ from those who live in a city, and both differ from those who live near the sea. There is also the influence of tradition to be taken into account : where there has been a long tradition of good religious instruction in a parish, the children will be much more teachable than those in a parish on a new housing estate, where there can be no tradition at all; children brought up in Christian homes will more readily grasp the inner meaning of what they are being taught than those from homes where religion has no place. Not only do children differ : teachers are as unlike each other as the children they teach. Some teachers will always be much more successful with certain methods than with others, whatever the children may be like; and they are usually better able to teach one age group than any of the others.

Teachers in organizations where religious instruction is given should, therefore, be willing—as so few are—to transfer to other departments when asked to do so, or, if they feel they are not making headway with their own class, they should ask to be transferred as soon as a vacancy occurs. It may be that a disheartened teacher in one department would be able to teach younger or older children with great success.

Teachers will also need to study their own children, and not assume they are everything that the text-book suggests they should be. Only personal experience can really teach the teacher how to teach. The suggestions made here are offered as sign-posts along the road, but it is for the teacher to decide which sign-post he should follow. This decision can only be made after patient and careful experiment : any one method needs to be tried over a fairly long period before it can definitely be pronounced a success or a failure; and children should be allowed to become thoroughly accustomed to one method before being introduced to another.

As this is not a lesson-book, actual lesson-notes for all the various subjects referred to have not been given. An attempt to do this might seem to suggest that there is a one and only right way in which to present a particular lesson, whereas there are probably as many different ways of doing so as there are different circumstances in which the lessons can be given. There is, however, a wide choice of lesson-books available for the parent or teacher who would like further guidance. Courses of lessons for all ages are published each year and these can be obtained from S.P.C.K. and other bookshops. The Mothers' Union also caters for the needs of parents who wish to give their children teaching suitable to their ages.

However useful such books and notes may be, they are not sufficient in themselves. A teacher should always know a good deal more about the subject he is teaching than he will necessarily pass on to the scholars, and this is particularly true where religious instruction is concerned. If we are to share with the children something wh'·h we possess in fuller measure than they, we must be ·   , sure that we do possess this fuller measure and not ¹   ·ntent merely to relay something out of a book.

The best guara·` · that our teaching will be sound is to be well grounded ourselves in the teaching and practice of the Church of which we are members. If we ourselves are well-instructed, then the children we teach will stand a good chance of being well-instructed, too! Much of the present vagueness about religion is probably due to the fact that i· the past many parents and teachers felt unable to give their children any definite religious teaching, because they themselves knew so little about the Faith they professed. Their children therefore grew up with still less knowledge, and also with considerable indifference to religion, and so had little or nothing to hand on to the present generation.

In order to give adequate religious instruction ·· `   ·   ·ɔ have a good knowledge of the Bible, not only from devotional reading, though this is important, but also from definite study aided by the reading of books written by Biblical scholars. Such reading should be systematic, and advice as to suitable books could be obtained from the parish clergy, or from leaders of religious education in the Diocese. We should also make ourselves familiar with the history, not only of the Early Church in the years immediately following the period covered by the New Testament, but also with that of the Church in England down to our own day; with the history and content of the Book of Common Prayer and not merely with the services we are accustomed to attend; and with the Doctrine of the Church which is summarized in the historic Creeds. Simple text-books have been written on all these subjects, and Public Libraries are always willing to

procure such books for members who make special request
for them.